Created in 2000 by

Virgin Books

An imprint of

Virgin Publishing Ltd

Thames Wharf Studios

Rainville Road

London W6 9HA

Text by Molly MacDermot

First published in the United States in 2000 by Billboard Books,

an imprint of Watson-Guptill Publications,

a division of BPI Communications Inc.,

at 770 Broadway, New York, NY 10003

www.watsonguptill.com

Library of Congress Cataloging in Publication data can be obtained from the

Library of Congress.

ISBN 0 8230 7866 3

Printed and bound in Spain

Set in Helvetica

Colour Origination by Colourwise Ltd

Designed by Balley Design Associates

First printing 2000

1 2 3 4 5 6 7 8 9/06 05 04 03 02 01 00

the unofficial book

britney spears

confidential

molly macdermot

BILLBOARD
BOOKS

Contents

Chapter One — Britney's Special Talent   6

Chapter Two — Tour Secrets 18

Chapter Three — The Steps Towards Stardom   34

Chapter Four — Dear Diary: Her Private Life 54

Chapter Five — Mama's Girl 66

Chapter Six — Video Magic 70

Chapter Seven — A Fan of Fashion   78

Chapter Eight — Hair and Make-up Tricks   82

Chapter Nine — Giving Back 86

Chapter Ten — Fast-Forward to the Future 90

Quiz 93

Discography 96

chapter one

Britney's Special Talent

She inspires us to reach for the stars. She makes us smile with song and dance. She reminds us that dreams are meant to be lived. She's Britney Jean Spears, the brown-eyed beauty who back-flipped into the music scene – and into our hearts – with boundless energy and enthusiasm. It's no wonder we're hooked on Britney. Ever since she hit us with the infectious song '… Baby One More Time' in late 1998, she has put smiles on our faces – and not all artists have that power.

What makes Britney a special talent – and a star who will continue to shine for years to come? She's passionate and positive with every performance that she gives. Whether she's jumping for joy with the get-up-and-move song 'Crazy' or quietly sitting on a bench belting out the heartfelt ballad 'From the Bottom of My Broken Heart', Britney knows how to deliver a memorable show that stays with the audience for days. As expressed in her song, she was born to make us happy, and, having sold more than 20 million albums worldwide, she has succeeded.

Her success story is inspirational and real. It's a story about a little girl with big goals, who went from small-town unknown to successful superstar.

And it's a story of how a winning combination of hard work, determination and luck can truly make your dreams come true. Just as she looked to Whitney Houston for inspiration when she sang the legendary hit 'I Have Nothing' for the demo tape that eventually landed Britney a record deal, fans have been looking to her for inspiration as they put together their own demo tapes to showcase their special talents.

This gutsy gal is blazing the path for her generation – her own way – just like Madonna, Mariah, Janet and Whitney did before her. Britney is proving that, although there will be other artists popping up who may challenge her record-breaking numbers and even beat them, there will always be just one Britney Spears.

Having scored hit after hit, Britney is arguably the most popular female artist of the new millennium so far, and she continues to hold that impressive title with her second chart-topping album *Oops! … I Did It Again*. With this second studio effort reaching multi-platinum status faster than her already record-breaking debut *…Baby One More Time* had, Britney proved that, yes, she did it again. She delivered yet another hit album, just a little more than a year after her first, and there's more to come.

She can't wait for her third album because she wants to bring her music to yet another level and surprise fans with new sounds.

Today, countless bedrooms across America are decorated with Britney memorabilia: posters, autographed photos, T-shirts, Britney dolls and more. Fans are singing Britney's words loud and clear, whether they're at her concerts, at their local karaoke clubs or in their own rooms; fans are also dressing up in tribute to their fave trendsetter, wearing the different outfits she sports in her videos for Halloween and costume parties. This stylin' sensation is also affecting beauty and fashion trends. While Jennifer Aniston's *Friends* hairdo was the most requested in salons during the 1990s, suddenly the actress has been replaced by Britney Spears, whose cool looks have made it on the 'most wanted' list for the millennium. There's even

a good chance that more teens own Britney albums than cell phones. Now that's a cool concept of which Britney would definitely approve.

It's not unusual to walk by a newsstand and see Britney's face splashed on several magazine covers. Her smile has launched a thousand newspaper and magazine articles; she is the second most searched item on the Internet behind Pokémon; she has a fashion line, Britney Jeans, and this sweet songbird even launched her own brand of bubble gum. Aside from music, Britney has television studios jockeying for her talents; she guest-appeared on *Sabrina* and also performed on *Saturday Night Live*, making her the first and youngest star to host and be a musical guest in the show's history. She spent a week rehearsing for her parts, which included, of all things, the role of a nerd. This multi-talented force has Hollywood knocking on her door, and she has said that she receives scripts frequently from producers who hope to get some of her time for a movie. Simply put, Britney is a hot commodity.

Who knew that this Southern belle from Kentwood, Louisiana, would blast out of nowhere and land at number one on the *Billboard* charts, *The Box* and MTV's *Total Request Live* countdown? Britney first woke up to the fact that she was number one on 19 January 1999, a week after the release of *...Baby One More Time*, when her lawyer and the president of her record company, Jive, called to tell her the amazing news.

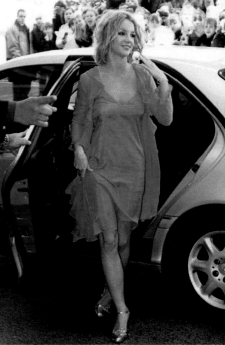

Britney's single and debut album had reached the number one position on the *Billboard* charts, making her the youngest artist ever to achieve this feat.

The fresh new face of pop music had just turned seventeen the month before. It was then that she stopped to thank her lucky stars because all that singing in the bathtub – as well as the incredible experience from *The New Mickey Mouse Club, Star Search* and her countless talent-show days – had prepared her for the dream of a lifetime. Britney was a star. Clearly, Britney's rapid rise to stardom has been a direct result of her dedication, as her childhood ambitions prove. She knew what she wanted at an early age, and used those dreams to propel her to perform.

How did she become so successful so quickly? Her love for music. One of Britney's earliest memories ever, not surprisingly, is a performance. She can picture it clearly: she was five years old singing 'What Child Is This' to her kindergarten classmates. She also remembers sitting in a New Orleans restaurant with her family when Otis Redding's song 'I've Been Loving You Too Long' came on the jukebox. She was moved and wanted to know more about the artist. The next day, her dad bought her *Otis Redding's Greatest Hits,* and since then she continues to draw inspiration from the legends.

One thing's for sure: Britney was a born performer who could carry a tune before she could form a sentence – and her family agree because they remember. When Britney's mother Lynne first listened to little Brinnie singing in the bathroom as a baby, she made a mental note to herself that her second-born had music in her future. Britney's brother Bryan – who is four years older than she is and has been studying sports administration at Southwest Mississippi Community College – remembers his eight-year-old younger sister prancing around the living room, disturbing his time watching television, as she belted out Madonna's 1989 hit 'Like a Prayer'. Even people living in the same street could hear the little tot belting lyrics from Michael Jackson's 'Thriller' from down the street. Britney remembers playing that Jackson tape so much she wore it out. Those were the days before CDs.

Britney's talents weren't restricted to the Spears house for long – after all, a star in the making jumps at the chance to perform before a public audience. She sang in the church choir, provided the entertainment at beauty pageants and basically volunteered her singing services wherever there was an available, listening audience. Kentwood witnessed the budding star shining in countless talent shows, winning her armfuls of trophies that still adorn her living-room shelf. Back when she was rehearsing Madonna-like mannerisms in the mirror and mimicking Janet Jackson's robotic rhythms, Britney knew that performing was what she wanted to do above everything – school, dolls, even sports. It came naturally to her. Visions of *Billboard* chart domination had not yet entered her mindset.

She was just happy to sing and dance for the fun of it, and that joy is what kept her going. Britney has said that she's always been her own stage mother and that no one has ever pushed her into showbiz.

What has unfolded for this determined girl still leaves her family, her friends and even the town of Kentwood shaking their heads in amazement. Britney is still the bubbly girl who likes to giggle over cute movie stars such as Ben Affleck, shop for wacky shoes such as purple cowboy boots, and chat on the cell phone until she has used up all of her minutes. However, she has grown a lot this last year and her life has changed incredibly since she embarked on her entertainment career almost a lifetime ago. When she was six, her claim to fame was winning first prize at the Kentwood Dairy Festival. Now, she's reached the point in her career where she's bringing home statuettes from the American Music Awards, the *Billboard* Awards, the MTV Awards and the Nickelodeon's Kids' Choice Awards. But, aside from winning awards, Britney has, more importantly, been winning fans. Even though she remembers singing into her hairbrush in front of the bathroom mirror as if it were just yesterday, she's leaped into the big league. Now she's singing into a microphone in front of a sold-out auditorium holding more than thirty thousand screaming fans.

Ever since Britney exploded on to the scene with her energetic, feel-good dance pop in 1999, a slew of new female solo artists have emerged with their own unique blend of new music, such as the powerful-piped Christina Aguilera, the romantic balladeer Jessica Simpson, the sweet-singing Mandy Moore and others who are putting the punch back into girl power. Britney and these other MTV regulars are showing the male artists – such as Enrique Iglesias, Blink-182, the guys from Backstreet Boys and 'N Sync – that there's more than enough room in the music world for everyone. In fact, many of today's artists – both the girls and the guys – are collaborating to make more music for their fans.

This fresh crop of newcomers – consisting mostly of teen talent – offers a refreshing change from the period during the 1990s when grunge, gangsta rap and angst-filled alternative anthems filled the charts.

The large population of teen listeners are looking to artists they can identify with, who are real. Britney has proved that she's a success – but that she's also human and fallible.

The only difference between Britney and her fans is that she made it, and it makes her fans realize that they can make it, too.

Even though critics are quick to lump the new female artists into the same category, savvy listeners know that Britney remains the reigning princess of pop for her generation. She has blazed a new path of music for other female solo artists, and she has said that she hopes to continue heading into the new millennium with the same energy and fun as her inspirations – Madonna, Mariah and Janet Jackson – achieved during the last decade. With the roots of her success firmly planted in both her determined personality and small-town sensibility, Britney proves you can be the most down-to-earth-girl on the planet and still reap superstar success.

What makes this humble girl next door so appealing to her fans? She's one of the hardest-working performers on the radio – Britney rarely gets a full night's sleep – and she delivers fresh material that other girls her age can relate to. Sometimes her lyrics are so modern that she leaves adults baffled. Britney's lyric 'Hit me, baby' is one example of her representing a different generation. Fans had to translate the hip phrase, which means give me a signal, to their parents. Her winning combination of upbeat music, energetic dance and stellar charisma seals her success. Most importantly, and what keeps her ego in check, is that she has never forgotten that she would not be where she is today if she didn't have the steady support of her fans.

When battling challenges, Britney stays strong. Along with her outpouring of fun-filled albums, videos and tours, Britney works hard at staying true to herself even when faced with the relentless gossip that accompanies fame. It takes a thick skin – and a belief in yourself – to stay afloat when the seas get stormy, and she's gone through hurricanes and back. The gossip mill has been working overtime on Britney, flooding

gossip columns with false tales that truly affect her. She has said that she's more sensitive and vulnerable than she lets on, and, while some stars can shrug off negative comments, Britney takes it to heart.

Idle chitchat about lip-syncing, feuds with fellow pop stars, artificial enhancements, public dissing by the rapper Eminem and romantic links with 'N Sync's Justin Timberlake and Prince William have left Britney hurt – and sympathetic fans frustrated. Although she wouldn't want to be doing anything other than living her dream as she is now, she has said that there are times when she is lonely.

In her hit single 'Lucky', she sings about a famous girl who appears to be larger than life, but who actually is quite human after all. In some respects, Lucky is not unlike Britney. The lyrics are revealing: 'But she cry, cry, cries in her lonely heart, thinking, If there's nothing missing in my life then why do these tears come at night?' In a live Internet chat, Britney talked about the single 'Lucky' and said, 'Even though ... it looks like you've got everything ... you don't really see friends and family ... everybody thinks that you're just having this big whoop-de-do time, but if you're really serious about the music business ... you can't play all the time, my gosh. You got to take it all seriously and work.'

Britney has said she misses taking walks, going to the mall and the movies and shopping alone. Downtime is rarely scheduled into her agenda. Britney's entourage causes such a sensation that she's had to avoid public places. When she goes to a hotel, she sneaks through the basement passageway, rarely setting foot in the lobby because her familiar face would cause too much commotion. When she's feeling overwhelmed by reporters and photographers, she tells her personal assistant and good friend Felicia Culotta, or 'Fee' as she likes to call her, 'It's stormy outside.' That's her code that says she needs time to be alone.

Being the true professional that she is, Britney has learned to keep her eye on what really matters: making music. She is not a diva complaining, but a gracious star embracing her success. What keeps her going is her ever-evolving fan base, and the ever-exciting future that is just beginning to unfold for this bright light. We don't know what the future holds for Britney, but, if the past is any indication, she is bound to bring us more songs to love.

Why we love Britney

(1) She accepts herself: Even though Britney thinks she has funny-looking toes and that her hair is too thin, and wishes she was taller than five foot four, she's learned it's important to embrace your own unique qualities. After all, it's cool to be different.

(2) She loves turkey sandwiches: Fame hasn't made this down-to-earth girl fancy frou-frou delicacies such as caviar and escargot. She still says nothing beats a turkey sandwich with cheese, lettuce, tomato, mayonnaise and mustard.

(3) She admits her fears: Britney has no problem performing in front of a packed crowd, but she does admit that she's afraid of the dark. She has said she feels as if something is going to jump out at her in the dark, so she always flicks the lights on. She's also panicky about flying, which can be an inconvenient fear because she's always on a plane flying from one country to the next.

(4) She believes in herself: Even when the tabloid press is churning out daily gossip about Britney, this strong girl sticks to her beliefs and rolls with the punches. She assures her fans that they can't believe everything they read and she hopes they'll see through the false tales.

(5) She cares: With fame comes responsibility – and Britney knows it. Based on her commitment to helping charities, she truly believes you have to give back when you've been blessed with good fortune. It also touches her heart.

(6) She's a trooper: When accidents happen, like the time she hurt her knee rehearsing for 'Sometimes' or when the metal piece of a camera fell on her head during the filming of the video for 'Oops!... I Did It Again', Britney manages to put her pain aside and perseveres so she can get the job done. Her motto is: 'Why feel sorry for yourself when you've got work to do?' Now that's a sure sign of a dedicated performer.

(7) She's close with her family: This superstar's days may be packed with press conferences, interviews, photo shoots, rehearsals and performances, but that doesn't stop Britney from phoning home on a daily basis. She insists on visiting her family in Kentwood at least every six weeks and makes sure she's involved in their lives. She has been known to fly home for her sister's softball games.

(8) She loves her fans: Few performers work as hard as Britney to produce new albums – she's had two in a just a little over a year – offer nonstop tours and talk with hundreds of fans during meet-and-greets and autograph signings. She has been known to meet with over two hundred people during one half-hour sitting. She tries to get in as many fans as possible. It's not uncommon for Britney to get as little as three hours' sleep a night because she prefers to spend her time doing what comes naturally to her: pleasing a crowd.

(9) She surprises us: Britney likes to experiment with different hair shades, styles, make-up looks and clothes so her fans always have something to look forward to. Like her idol, Madonna, Britney knows it's important to keep growing artistically if she wants to keep her fans interested. If the millions of Britney supporters around the world are anything to go by, she's succeeding.

(10) She cherishes her friendships: When Britney is home, she calls up her close pals to catch up on news. They go shopping, rent videos or just sit and talk for hours. Sometimes when they were younger, they would play Truth or Dare. One time, Britney was dared to eat a messy mixture of mashed cheese, raw eggs and sauces. Never one to pass up a challenge, she held her nose and gulped down the gross combination of food.

Confidential essentials

- full name: **Britney Jean Spears**
- nickname: **Boo**
- born in: **Kentwood, Louisiana, USA**
- parents: **Jamie and Lynne**
- date of birth: **2 December 1981**
- sign: **Sagittarius**
- compatible with: **Leo, Gemini, Taurus**
- eyes: **Brown**
- hair: **Light brown**
- birth order: **Middle child of three siblings. She has an older brother Bryan, and younger sister Jamie Lynn**
- she writes with her: **Right hand**
- she's scared of: **The dark**
- she's weak for: **Romance novels by Jackie Collins and Danielle Steel, and cookie-dough ice cream**
- her fave movie: *Steel Magnolias*
- her fave energy booster: **Mocha cappuccino**
- the old-fashioned movie she loves: **Audrey Hepburn's 1961 classic** *Breakfast at Tiffany's*
- her friend and chaperone on the road: **Felicia Culotta**
- what she did on her break between albums: **Had her wisdom teeth removed**
- fave childhood hobby: **Riding her go-cart**

Superstar stats

(1) Britney has sold more than 20 million albums – and counting – around the world. That means more than twice the number of people living in New York City own her album.

(2) She's the first – and youngest – female artist to simultaneously have the number one single on the *Billboard* 100 and the number-one album on the *Billboard* 200 charts for her debut *... Baby One More Time*.

(3) When Britney took home four trophies at the 1999 MTV Europe Awards, she became the first single nominee to win all the awards she was nominated for: Best Female Artist, Best Breakthrough Artist, Best Pop Artist, Best Pop Song. For Best Female Artist she beat out Lauryn Hill and Madonna; for Best Pop Artist, she topped Backstreet Boys and Ricky Martin; for Best Breakthrough Artist she beat out Jennifer Lopez and Eminem; for Best Pop Song for '... Baby One More Time' she beat Madonna, TLC and the Backstreet Boys.

(4) All of Britney's released singles have sold more than a million units, and all of her videos have become the top requests on MTV's *Total Request Live*. In fact, the day after 'Oops! ...I Did It Again' hit stores, it was made the number-one requested video on Total Request Live by her loyal fan base.

(5) Her second album beat the sales pace of her first album. Less than a month after its sophomore debut, *Oops! ... I Did It Again* was certified four times platinum for selling 4 million copies by the Recording Industry Association of America. ... Baby One More Time was certified double platinum a month after its debut – which is still a giant feat considering it was an unknown artist's debut.

(6) *Oops! ... I Did It Again* sold 1,319,000 copies in its first week in stores, scoring the biggest single sales week for a female artist in SoundScan history and landing Britney at number one on the *Billboard* 200. The previous holder for the most units sold in its first week was Alanis Morissette's *Supposed Former Infatuation Junkie* with 469,054, and in any one week by a female artist was Mariah Carey with *Daydream*, which sold 759,959 during the Christmas week in 1995.

(7) *Oops! ... I Did It Again* debuted at number one around the world, including Canada, Japan, Germany, Sweden and France.

(8) Britney is the second most popular item searched on the Internet, trailing closely behind Pokémon, but beating out the Japanese cartoon Dragonball.

(9) The series of Britney Spears dolls was one of the most popular toys on the list for *ToyFare* magazine's 'Hottest 25 Toys' for the year 2000. Other toys on the list included those based on *The Simpsons* and *South Park*.

(10) Britney's debut *... Baby One More Time* came in as the second best-selling album of 1999 behind the Backstreet Boys' *Millennium*. Her album went to number one in fifteen countries and was certified Diamond by the music industry, which means it sold more than 10 million copies.

Tour Secrets

Britney is a born performer, so the larger her audience the better. That's why it's not surprising that she loves touring around the world to sold-out stadiums. Whether she's sweeping across the entire United States and up into Canada, or flying oceans away to Europe or Asia, Britney is a frequent flyer, globetrotting on a monthly basis. She delights in discovering new lands, new cultures, new foods and above all new fans. Britney has said that it's rewarding to talk with fans from around the world; it's truly her time to personally connect with the people who listen to her music.

Of course, life on the road isn't always a smooth ride: Britney has had to learn how to sleep on a bumpy bus and find things to keep her busy for long stretches of time as she makes her way from one city to the next. It's not unusual for her driver, JT, to hit the road for at least fifteen hours straight to get from one state to the next in time for a performance. Sometimes the bus stops at a hotel in the middle of the night to unload Britney and the crew for a few hours' sleep before pushing off again on the endless highway. Other times, there are no more flights available and Britney has little choice but to drive to her next destination by bus.

For Britney, there's no bigger thrill than watching fans' faces during a song and seeing them singing along to every word.

With the bright spotlights shining into the audience, Britney can scan the faces of her fans to check on the vibe.

She always knows if it's a good show or not from the fans' reactions. Always the perfectionist, Britney uses what she learns from each show to better the next one. Surprisingly, Britney is secretly quite shy, but has learned to speak up more to develop a rapport with her audience, instead of letting the singing and dancing do the talking. Now, it's not uncommon for her to scream out questions to the audience, like 'Are you having a good time? I can't hear you.'

Britney will never forget her very first mini-tour back when she was sixteen and still new to the whole showbiz world. Having just recorded her debut album, with its release still months away, Britney kicked off a 28-date promotional mall tour at summer's end in 1998. Nervous about presenting her music publicly for the first time, as any new artist would be, Britney bravely performed her four-song routine

with two backup dancers in shopping malls across the US. The response was tremendous; people were intrigued by her and wanted to know more about this fresh, new talent who was wowing them with her combination of song and dance. It didn't take long for a buzz to generate, as word of mouth got around that there was a cool new kid on the block. By the time her single '... Baby One More Time' was released on 23 October 1998, there was already a growing fan base – Britney was on the brink of becoming a star.

Tour life has changed dramatically for Britney since that mall gig in 1998. For starters, she's not as nervous about performing, and has become used to seeing the crowds with their posters and homemade signs fluttering throughout the stadium.

She's discovered that she will never again wonder what it is like to be loved by her fans.

Now that she's performing in her own elaborate headlining tours and singing and dancing to her hit songs in huge stadiums around the world, Britney can't help but feel amazed. Her shows have blown up into elaborate productions that Britney had only dreamed about. Now that she's been touring for over two years, she's much more comfortable presenting her music. She's also been touring with the same people for so long that she's grown to love them like family.

In a nutshell, a Britney Spears concert is pure fun. Experiencing Britney live gives you an unmistakable adrenaline rush – and it's hard to fall asleep later without replaying the evening's show in your head. Can you imagine how hard it must be for Britney to wind down? As soon as she says goodbye to the crowd, she sprints on the tour bus parked behind the stadium, and, still out of breath from the performance, she tries to get in a good night's sleep before doing the same thing all over again the following day. Quite simply, tour life for Britney is like running a marathon.

A typical concert begins around 8 p.m., about the time fans flock to their seats in the sold-out stadium – which can often hold up to fifty thousand people. Britney's opening acts get the audience revved up with their own blend of new music. A number of talented groups and solo acts have graced the stage during Britney's sold-out tours, such as the British trio BBMak, Steps, Five, Nobody's Angel, 2gether – the spoof boy band from MTV – and the girl group Innosense. Incidentally, Britney had originally joined Innosense before pursuing a solo career. Another interesting fact is that Justin Timberlake's mother, Lynn Harless, manages Innosense. Countless other artists who have opened for her have all contributed in their own way to making a Britney concert complete. For the lucky supporting groups who are chosen for such a huge tour, it's a major career boost to snag such a highly coveted spot. It gives them that tremendous exposure to reach a mainstream audience. Britney remembers feeling privileged – and lucky – when she landed the opening gig on the 'N Sync tour in late 1998. It was a once-in-a-lifetime opportunity to reach out to thousands of potential fans.

Once the final opening act wraps up their last song at a Britney concert, the fans' cheers begin to build and, before long, everyone is standing up for the wave: that's when rows and rows of audience members jump up with their hands held high to create a falling-domino effect. Growing more and more impatient to see their star emerge from backstage, the audience begin screaming the name that was invented for chanting, 'Brit-*ney!* Brit-*ney!*'

As the sun sets, fans wave their glow sticks in the night air, creating the effect of a fluorescent green sea filling the stadium. Permeating the air are the sweet-smelling candy and buttery popcorn smells wafting from the concession stands. Gaudy beach balls bounce from one fan's outreached hand to the next. Some creative supporters dress up for the show wearing looks inspired by Britney's videos, such as her sassy school uniform in '… Baby One More Time', her sparkling green tube top in 'Crazy' and her head-to-toe white get-up in 'Sometimes'. Dressing like Britney is a way for fans to pay tribute to their stylin' star.

Some concertgoers come to the show with armloads of flowers, notes and care packages in the hope of hand-delivering their gifts backstage to the star of the evening.

There's not one person in the crowd who isn't desperate to meet Britney up close. Some lucky fans have won tickets to attend the meet-and-greets with Britney before the concert.

Others keep their fingers crossed that they'll get their own glimpse of the star coming out of her tour bus. Britney is usually welcomed by a group of excited fans waiting by the gates for her arrival. After slowing down so as not to hurt anyone, the bus peels into the restricted-parking area behind the stage so Britney can hop off and start preparing for the show. It's easy to figure out if Britney is in town because her entourage includes at least ten buses to transport the band, the dancers and the rest of her 'dream team', as she calls it.

As the excitement grows in the stadium, Britney pumps herself up backstage for her grand entrance. Everyone is sitting on the edge of their seat trying to guess which Britney hit will start the evening. Will it be the get-out-of-your-seat-and-dance song 'Crazy'? Or will she treat the audience to '…Baby One More Time' from the get-go? Then the topic turns to Britney's clothes. What will this fashion diva wear next? Will it be a crop-top made of silver sequins? Or will she float on stage engulfed in fluffy white boa feathers, as she has in the past?

Just when the fans can't stand the suspense another second, Britney's five-piece band, made up of Skip, Freddy, Slam, Dan and Mike, take their cue and build the bass to a pounding rhythm, echoing a heartbeat. Britney's band keep a low profile, but she graciously thanked them in the liner notes of *Oops! ... I Did It Again.* She wrote that they're 'five of the best guys whom I couldn't do without'.

Just as the screams reach jet-engine proportions, the fans finally get what they've been waiting for. Britney emerges on stage. For over an hour and a half, fans are transported to Britney's world of set transformations, complicated dance routines and enough smash songs to satisfy the tens of thousands of fans. Britney often gives an encore, thanks the audience and then – whoosh! – the evening is over.

This is just a glimpse of one of Britney's shows, but, as every true concert fan knows, nothing beats witnessing this pop princess with your own two eyes. It's her talent for performing that makes her tours some of the most celebrated and successful musical events in history. Her shows get sold out in minutes and fans have been known to do anything for tickets, including camping out for days in freezing cold weather.

Following the release of her second album, Britney kicked off her 'Oops! ... I Did It Again' summer tour and performed to one of her largest audiences yet, selling out 20,000-plus-seat stadiums from New York to California in a flash.

The tour had lots of surprises, for both the fans and Britney. For starters, Britney, who always travels with an eight-person dance team, replaced three of her dancers on the tour with Ryan, Bryan and Gil, who danced with Janet Jackson. Her previous dancers, Andre, TJ and Alex, who had been working with Britney from the very beginning, left to advance their careers with new creative projects. Although Britney remains close to her original dancers, it was an emotional time when she had to say goodbye to a part of her team who had been with her from the beginning.

Britney has a good eye for picking amazing dancers, and it didn't take long for fans to applaud the new guys for their gravity-defying flips and fancy footwork.

Another surprise came from Britney: she decided it was time for her own tour bus. With all the pressure riding on the new album and its tour, Britney took every step to make sure she was in top form. That would require her to get the essential downtime she needed to recharge her battery for each night's performance. For her previous tours, she has shared a bus with her dancers and had special times with them talking to all hours of the night, playing cards or watching movies. She knew that she needed a change and set out to create a home away from home. After all, she spends most of her time on a tour bus – so she decided it was time to decorate the bus to make it feel more like her own home. Another inside scoop: Britney fills her bus with huge lollipops, which have become a fave tour treat.

One day, she went with her 350-pound bodyguard and her assistant, Felicia, to Wal-Mart to pick up some bedroom essentials: throw pillows, a bedspread, a blanket, a rug, some candles, a few lace doilies and little lamps. She decorated her home on wheels in soothing lavender shades. She has said that it's important to make your space comfortable and homey or you can feel like a lost soul.

Britney even has a sun bed on the bus for instant tanning and relaxation when she's on the go. She uses her bus as her sanctuary, a place where she can be away from all the craziness that comes with her famous life. One of her fave things to do after a long day is to put on Macy Gray's album, *On How Life Is*, light soft candles and draw a warm, bubbly bath for instant calm.

It may seem that Britney is far enough in her career that she's over stage fright, but, secretly, artists almost always feel the jitters before a show, and Britney is no exception. She has said that she was really nervous about the tour for the new album because not only was it an elaborate production but she had the whole world watching. After all, she was presenting her second studio effort to the world, and, as music insiders know, a sophomore album hot on the heels of a successful debut can make or break an artist. Always one to stare challenges in the face, Britney devoted her weeks leading up to the tour with nonstop rehearsals to get her dance routines and songs perfect. Of course, once she had her first show of the tour, which was on 20 June 2000 in Merriweather Post in Columbia, Maryland, Britney was psyched. Unfortunately, she had to cancel some shows because the stage didn't accommodate all of her sets and special-effects contraptions. She has said that she felt pumped for the rest of the shows and that the audiences' screams filled her body with a really good energy, which stayed with her until the last show at the Coca-Cola Lakewood Amphitheater in Atlanta, Georgia, in September.

The 53-date sizzling summer tour for *Oops! ... I Did It Again* included other surprise stage additions.

Massive video screens above the stage showed a computerized version of Britney welcoming everyone to the event and a montage of Britney images followed on the effects-laden video screen. The show began with a poof of pyro and the flash of hundreds of synchronized lights. Descending on to the stage in a hovering spaceship, Britney emerged, flanked by her eight dancers.

Britney has said that the 'Oops! ... I Did It Again' tour reminded her of an elaborate Broadway show. A cartoon-like *Alice in Wonderland* bedroom set complete with an oversized teddy bear lent a playful background to the evening. There was even a pillow fight and a moment when Britney and the dancers squirted everyone with water pistols. Numerous costume changes had to be quick, so Britney did a lot of her disrobing behind a screen on the stage. She even tumbled through a tunnel of fire during her blazing performance of 'Oops! … I Did It Again'.

At one point, the video screen above the stage flashed back on and the five familiar faces that make up 'N Sync introduced an audience-participation game. Justin Timberlake, Lance Bass, Joey Fatone, JC Chasez and Chris Fitzpatrick announced that someone in the audience would have the chance to meet Britney. With the help of Britney's backup singers, four members of the audience were invited on stage to play the game, which required the contestants to sing, dance and act super-silly in front of the packed arena. Before the goofy game was over, both the contestants on stage and the audience were roaring with laughter. As always, a Britney extravaganza requires a sense of fun.

One of the highlights of the evening was Britney standing at the top of a spiral staircase wearing a gorgeous long white dress covered in boa feathers that trailed thirty feet down a flight of stairs for one of her fave power ballads from the new album, 'Don't Let Me Be the Last to Know'. She has said that the soaring ballad, written for her by the husband-and-wife team Mutt Lange and Shania Twain, is a pure and delicate tune that instantly pulls you in. It's also a good song to showcase Britney's vocal strengths. During a gravity-defying moment, she performed her remake of Sonny and Cher's 'The Beat Goes On' atop a platform that lifts high above the stage, making her look as if she was standing on super-long stilts, like clowns in the circus.

Her encore is usually the highly anticipated girl anthem '… Baby One More Time'. Britney changed into several outfits throughout the song, including a school uniform and a cheerleading costume. Bags full of red and white confetti filled the air and the whole arena looked like the site of a huge sporting event.

Britney's past tours have been equally as cool, as her fans can confirm. 'Cool' seems to be a frequent word used by fans to describe her shows. In March 2000, the 'You Drive Me Crazy' spring tour swept across the US, starting in Florida, with artists such as LFO and Bosson opening up the show. The tour was a great success, with Britney flying on a magic carpet and basically serving up what she does best: non-stop music and dancing.

Fans will always remember Britney's very first headlining tour for '… Baby One More Time' during the summer of 1999. The 51-city tour spanned from June to September, with C-Note, Michael Fredo, PYT and Steps, among others, opening for her. Britney sang her hits, including '… Baby One More Time', 'From the Bottom of My Broken

Heart' and 'Sometimes'. She also paid homage to her idols with covers of Madonna's spirited song 'Material Girl' and two of Janet Jackson's hits, 'Black Cat' and 'Nasty'. She had one rule during the tour: they had to have fun, and she expressed that sentiment with her bold, striking costumes. She wore a hot-pink leather-look tube top and shiny and white vinyl pants along with other hotter-than-lava fashion statements.

The tour Britney will never forget was back in the autumn of 1998 when she joined 'N Sync as their opening act. It was the first of many things for Britney: the first time she was away from home since landing a record deal; the first time she was opening a concert before thousands of people; the first time she was touring with her old friends, JC Chasez and Justin Timberlake, from *The New Mickey Mouse Club*. The guys had changed since she first met them six years earlier. They were older now, and famous. Instead of chanting 'M-I-C-K-E-Y M-O-U-S-E' with them, Britney was joining the guys on a giant tour that showcased their music. 'N Sync had blown up into such a popular phenomenon she was afraid she wouldn't fit in. Also, she faced the tough task of winning over the crowd. A confessed worrier, Britney feared she would forget her dance steps or flub the words in a song. Naturally, the tour went on without a hitch and 'N Sync made Britney feel truly a part of their team. She realized Justin and JC really hadn't changed that much. They were just older, and more focused, like herself.

Britney remembers the challenges of being a female performer opening for a popular male group like 'N Sync. She would rush out on stage only to hear the girls screaming the guys' names. She has said she only hoped they would give her a chance, and sure enough, by the time she was into the second song of her set, the audience warmed up to the newcomer and began changing their tune by chanting 'Britney'. Even though she saw 'N Sync only during rushed lunches and dinners, and a few minutes here and there backstage, the guys joked around with her in that comforting way that made her feel truly welcomed. Britney will never forget their generosity and kindness during that tour. In fact, when she celebrated her seventeenth birthday on 2 December 1998, the fabulous five took the time out of their hectic schedule to surprise Britney on her tour bus with a birthday cake. She was even treated to a special, harmonized version of 'Happy Birthday' from the soulful singers. That day holds a special place in Britney's heart because it was also the day she found out that her single for '… Baby One More Time' had gone gold, selling 500,000 copies in one day. Needless to say, Britney spent that memorable moment celebrating.

It finally hit her: people liked her music and were going out to buy it.

Since that memorable tour with 'N Sync, Britney has had the chance to perform with the group on other occasions, such as award shows. Unfortunately, not all those memories are good ones. When Britney performed before 'N Sync at MTV's Video Music Awards in September 1999, the host for the evening, Chris Rock, quipped (falsely) that Britney and 'N Sync were lip-syncing, to a stunned and uncomfortable audience. What could have been a perfect night in the Metropolitan Opera House, where the award show took place, was blemished by the rude remark. On top of that, she lost. She was nominated for Best Pop Video, Best Female Video and Best Choreography, and lost to Ricky Martin, Lauryn Hill and Fatboy Slim, respectively.

Harsh comments come and go but for Britney they can hurt for a long time. She has said that she and 'N Sync had worked hard for that live performance, singing and dancing their butts off, and that it was totally uncool, and unfair, to be insulted like that on national television. Britney has said that she understands how people could misinterpret her singing as lip-syncing. Britney has cleared up the tittle-tattle over lip-syncing by pointing out that, during her tour, the big screen above the stage is actually showing delayed footage of Britney, so the image isn't in sync with the music.

Another point she makes is that, when she's dancing hard on stage, the sound technicians sometimes up the volume of the background vocals to fill the gaps when Britney is spinning in midair and can't deliver her notes as strongly. She has a signal she gives them that lets the sound studio know she's out of breath and needs help. Clearly, singing and dancing at the same time isn't easy, especially when you're busting out moves the way Britney does. Up until Britney hit the music scene, most performers relied on their backup dancers to do the tough moves while they stood by their microphones. Pushing away convention, Britney breaks the rules and leads the dancers in unison with moves that have been inspired by dance pros such as Janet Jackson. In fact, Janet has attended a Britney show to check out her choreography.

After completing her North American leg of the 'Oops' tour in Atlanta, Georgia, Britney had less than a month to relax before starting her international tour, which hit much of Europe, focusing mostly on Britain. There were plans for 'N Sync to join Britney for a British tour in the autumn of 2000, but it was called off. Because 'N Sync's own US tour was so successful they decided to remain on their home turf and add more tour dates. It would have been a nostalgic tour reunion for everyone, but they are planning other collaborative projects for the future. A point of interest is that Britney's breaks between tours are brief: she sometimes has just a few weeks before starting new tours, which is not surprising from a workaholic such as Britney.

Britney enjoys meeting her international fans and told her audience at the Kokusai Forum Hall in Tokyo that she was so thankful for their support – and impressed that they knew all the English words to the songs. For an American artist steeped in pop tradition, gaining equal popularity in Europe is an added bonus. For Britney, the cool thing about performing is that it's spontaneous: she feeds off the audiences' vibe. Some nights she's said she feels much more on than other nights, and she's the first to admit she has had a low-energy show, even when everyone around her is gushing. There are always those moments, however, when a performance suddenly takes a wrong turn, causing endless embarrassment.

Britney is no stranger to humiliating moments in public and has had to deal with sudden disasters that left her wishing she was invisible.

When she was first on the road for her promotional mall tour in the summer of 1998, someone had accidentally left a cupcake on the stage and Britney's foot slid from under her. To her horror, the singer went flying and landed flat on the stage. With the help of her dancers, Britney was able to get right back up and finish the song without missing a beat. She's also lost her headset during a song, which made it hard to follow the music and continue singing. One time Britney tried to cover up a pimple with brown eyeliner so it would look like a beauty mark, but after a few high-energy dance routines on stage, the sweat from her face smeared the make-up all over. She's had continual costume catastrophes – buttons popping, splits, jackets that wouldn't come off when she had to make an on-stage outfit change. But Britney's learned to go with the flow. Naturally, red-in-the-face fiascos are unavoidable, so Britney has learned to laugh off the mortifying moments and continue like a professional.

Hop on the tour bus

You know what it is like to see a Britney show, but what would it be like if you had your very own backstage pass? Or, better yet, a personal invite to join Britney on tour? If you hopped on the bus, you'd be pulled into a whirlwind of little sleep, lots of work, and tons of excitement. Your day would start around 6 a.m., the time Britney has had to start interviews, specifically on-air radio chats, and sometimes end the day as late as 2 a.m. Your mornings would be spent studying with Britney: she's about to complete her last few high school correspondence classes through the University of Nebraska. Then there would be more interviews for Britney, either on the phone or in person. She may even have to do several back-to-back magazine photo shoots. Eating on tour is always rushed, so you'd probably wolf down a turkey sandwich for lunch, Britney's fave.

During the afternoon, you would join Britney on a trip to the venue where that evening's performance will be held. Most of her concerts take place in outside auditoriums or arenas that hold thousands of people. It's an amazing feeling to stand at the edge of the stage and look out on all the rows of seats. Before any members of the audience arrive at the location, Britney does a sound check to smooth over last-minute kinks before the performance. By 6 p.m., Britney goes to her dressing room, puts on her fluffy pink robe and sits still for an hour while a stylist carefully does her hair and make-up, making sure it's flawless for the fans in the front row.

It's a backstage fact that Britney reserves an hour of quiet time for herself before a big show – and only close friends and her family are allowed to disturb her. She carries around an impressive CD collection that she listens to in her dressing room. If you perused her albums, you'd find music from Madonna, Janet Jackson, Prince, Backstreet Boys, 'N Sync, Monica, TLC, Corrs, Blackstreet and others. Her current musical tastes, which are constantly expanding, take in pop, R&B, rock and more. To get pumped before dashing on stage, Britney blasts a fast song. For inspiration, she listens to Whitney Houston because she has said the diva belts out her songs with all her heart. She also keeps her stamina up by eating high-energy foods, and she always has a glass of hot water with lemon and honey handy to soothe her throat. Sometimes, right before she's about to give a performance, Britney has been known to go into a quiet room and scream at the top of her lungs until her voice opens up.

There are more rituals. Britney gives thanks right before every performance by joining hands with her dancers to say a prayer. It's difficult to get to church every Sunday when she's on the road, so this Southern Baptist keeps her prayer journal, or her Bible book, as she calls it, with her at all times. She finds peace in writing down her thoughts at the end of each day. That is also the time she's inspired to write down melodies she's been playing with, or poems that come to her. Often, writing in her journal helps her fall asleep, she has said.

Starting the first leg of a tour means that Britney's already crazy lifestyle will switch to an even faster pace.

She has to eat on the go, live out of a suitcase and fight off the nagging feelings of loneliness. Although Britney is rarely alone, that doesn't mean she's not lonely. Because of her soaring fame, she has said that it's difficult to go anywhere – even just a walk with her dog or a trip to the nearest Abercrombie & Fitch – without her security chaperoning; when Britney is out in public it's intense. Of course, she puts her foot down once in a while and insists on her independence, like the time she went to Hawaii to perform her televised concert. She was determined to take a leisurely stroll on the beach – without anyone accompanying her – so she did. Of course, her bodyguard, Big Rob, wasn't too pleased. When she finally did get her bodyguard to agree, Britney has said that she read her book for a whole two hours uninterrupted; she also burned to a crisp in the sun and has said she ended up looking like a lobster. Britney really cherishes any freedom she gets.

Battling loneliness on the road is a constant chore for most touring artists, and Britney is no exception. What keeps her going? For starters, Britney is close with her dancers: they play cards and board games, watch videos and talk for hours. They're her dependable support team, as is her chaperone and friend on the road, Felicia, or 'Fee', Culotta. She has said Fee is her surrogate mother when she's on the road, looking out for Britney the way her own mother would if she could travel with her all the time. The two spend every waking moment together, whether they're backstage, attending magazine photo shoots or interviews, or speaking with management about upcoming projects and business matters.

Fee, who worked as a children's dental hygienist near Kentwood before becoming Britney's best friend on the road, met Britney's mother more than ten years ago. She was invited to see Britney perform and recently revealed that she was amazed by the tiny performer.

In September 1997, Britney's mother called Fee, asking if she would travel with and assist Britney for a few months; Britney had just landed her record deal a few months before and was going through the process of putting together an album and preparing for a stretch of time far from home. Those few months turned into years, and now, after everything that has happened, they've become very close. Britney has said

that Fee keeps her grounded, humble and sane.

Clearly, that close bond with Fee has helped Britney cope with the crazy twists and turns of showbiz life. Fee provides her with guidance, honest feedback and a shoulder to cry on when life gets tough.

Another way Britney beats the blues from tour life is by keeping in constant touch with her family, no matter how busy she is. Ultimately, it's her passions, her family and the inspiring affection from her fans that keep Britney going.

Britney takes over the tube

With fame come television duties, so Britney has taken on the daunting task of speaking and performing before millions of viewers on live national television. This can be an especially difficult feat if she's tired from just coming off a plane or has finished a late show the night before, but Britney has learned how to put her exhaustion aside and face the cameras with poise and grace. Of course, she's had lots of television training from her days on *The New Mickey Mouse Club* and from performances on *Star Search*. Now she works the talk-show circuit: she's appeared on *The Rosie O'Donnell Show*, *The Tonight Show With Jay Leno*, *The Late Show With David Letterman* and others. She's also presented and accepted awards numerous times on television before the world. It's at these televised award shows that Britney gets to meet her inspirations up close. She has said she positively freaks when she sees Mariah Carey or Whitney Houston next to her. Even though her fans may be just as thrilled to be up close to her, Britney feels the same way about the artists she respects.

She has guest-appeared on the actress Melissa Joan Hart's show *Sabrina*, provided her voice for the cartoon comedy, *The Simpsons,* and guest-hosted on the comedy variety show, *Saturday Night Live,* which was one of her most challenging – and rewarding – stints on TV. She did such a good acting job that she generated a buzz in Hollywood: could she be the next A-list actress on the big screen?

She's also performed televised concerts around the world, such as the one in Waikiki, Hawaii, which was taped on 24 April 2000 for the television special show *Britney in Hawaii* for Fox TV. Hordes of fans – ten thousand of them – packed the waterside in what was one of the largest concerts they've ever had on the beach, and it was free. The roads in and out of the beach were gridlocked with bumper-to-

bumper traffic for hours, so plucky fans parked where they could and walked up to a mile to get to the concert. The audience were treated to a two-hour concert that boasted fireworks, special effects and exciting performances. The three-member R&B group Destiny's Child came on stage to sing their take-a-stand song 'Say My Name'. Then Britney's dancers came out individually and danced one-by-one to a song of their choice, such as N Sync's 'Bye Bye Bye' and Ricky Martin's 'Livin' La Vida Loca'. Earlier, Britney had met with a hundred lucky fans for a traditional *luau* – a feast of Hawaiian food.

Aside from performing television concerts, Britney has plans in motion for her own television show. She'd been in talks to make appearances on the hit television show *Dawson's Creek,* but Britney's busy year has left her with little time to fly to North Carolina, where the show is taped. It would have been a bonus to see her appear with the show's stars, Katie Holmes, Joshua Jackson and James Van Der Beek. Television is still an option in Britney's future. Her development deal with Columbia TriStar could easily yield a television show for Britney – there's been such success with pop stars making the crossover to the small screen. Brandy is the perfect example of a crossover artist because she has put out albums, starred in movies, such as *I Still Know What You Did Last Summer,* and tried television by joining the cast of the TV show *Moesha.* Mandy Moore is another personality who is dipping her toes in both music and television and even landed her own show on MTV, *Mandy.* It won't be long before Britney does the same thing with her own brand of style. We'll keep our fingers crossed for Britney's own television show debut.

chapter three

The Steps Towards Stardom

When Britney cruises up to Carson Daly on MTV's *Total Request Live* to chat about her new hit video of the moment, or saunters on stage to accept yet another music award, it seems as if she has always been a pop star. It's easy to forget that Britney has actually been working long and hard to reach this point in her career. Although critics are quick to call her an overnight sensation, it's actually taken her a lifetime – ever since she was a mere babe singing to her mother. Way before she became a blip on the music radar, she was rehearsing her dance routines relentlessly in an empty dance studio, or rehearsing her notes alone in her room while other kids her age were playing video games and watching television.

Even though she's considered remarkably young next to her more established peers who have been in the business for decades, those close to her know the truth:

This ambitious artist has actually been preparing herself for stardom ever since she was a little kid listening to Michael Jackson and Madonna at home in Kentwood.

So who is the real Britney? That question can be answered by going back to her roots. When Britney came into the world on 2 December 1981, it didn't take long for her parents, Jamie and Lynne, to figure out that their baby girl was destined to be an entertainer. Her mother has said that she still remembers the distinct singing issuing from Britney's lips when she was a tiny baby. Even though her dad, a building contractor, and her mother, a schoolteacher, weren't professional artists themselves, they appreciated the arts and filled the home with music, exposing their children to an eclectic blend of artists. It wouldn't be unusual to walk down the Spears family's tree-lined street and hear singing coming from their three-bedroom ranch-style house.

Little Brinnie would spend hours in the backyard jumping on the trampoline, hitting high notes with every bounce she made. Before long, the living room was taken over by Britney's balance beam so she could put her energies into gymnastics. When family friends came over she treated her guests to a gymnastic performance.

Lynne knew her tireless daughter needed an outlet for her energies, so she enrolled her in ballet class at Renée Donewar's School of Dance, an hour away from Kentwood in New Orleans. It was in that small studio that Britney took her first dance steps. In fact, those standard ballet positions have provided the foundation for Britney's now complicated choreography. If you watch her steps carefully, you can see her feet, legs and arms following the ballet training that was drilled into her from an early age.

Britney's dance teacher noticed that her student was a natural after just a few classes and she told Lynne that her daughter was a talented girl who could not only dance but also sing. It's her versatility for song and dance that solidifies Britney's successful performances and has allowed her to rise above the competition. The teacher recommended that Britney explore her talents with recitals and local shows. Britney did just that, performing at any event that came up, including Berry Day, a talent show that allows Kentwood talents an outlet for their creativity.

Two years of dance class only whetted her appetite for more and before long Britney was diving head first into gymnastics class, where she learned many of the moves she now displays in her videos, such as her jaw-dropping tumbles and back flips. Even as a kid, Britney had a strong work ethic, so, once school was over for the year and summer kicked in, she knew she needed a challenge. She begged her parents to let her train in Houston under the famous Olympic gymnastics coach Bela Karolyi, who fashioned the legendary Nadia Comaneci into a winner of Olympic gold.

Today, Britney's passions continue to drive her to perfection – she's tireless about rehearsing her steps and songs, as her crew know – and she was no different growing up. In fact, she would cry buckets of tears if she had to miss gymnastics class; she refused to fail at anything she put her mind to. But after struggling to reach the top Britney realized she was not destined to be the future gymnastics star at the Olympics. Her talents were forged in the specific combination of dance and song; it made sense that she make the switch from the gym floor to the stage. Even at eight, Britney was on the track to becoming the multi-talented performer she wanted to be. Surprisingly, Britney admits she has a shy side, but those early days of talent competitions and weekly performances in the church choir gave

her the confidence to perform publicly. Now, she draws from the wealth of knowledge that she gained from these experiences. This is especially true when she has to get on stage and perform a song during an event as big as the 42nd Annual Grammy Awards.

Although she still gets nervous before a big crowd, she's learned how to dodge potential pitfalls and face the world head on by working hard on her material and believing in herself.

The constant – one thing Britney continues to excel at – is that she performs well under pressure.

Growing up in a small town has also boosted Britney's creativity. She had the peace and quiet to work on her own unique style without many distractions or outside influences. Britney has joked that there are lots of cows in her quiet hometown, and not much else. The nearest McDonald's is fifteen minutes away by car and the mall is at least an hour away. To her benefit, she had the time to imagine her dreams. She remembers many instances when she would gaze out of the window, deep in thought, picturing herself performing for a large audience.

Her small-town upbringing meant close ties with fellow residents, and it wasn't uncommon for folks to stop by the Spears household for a friendly chat and delivery of home-baked goods such as Mississippi Mud Pie. In fact, she could just skip next door to visit her grandparents for heart-to-heart talks and a slice of apple pie. Britney has said that everyone in Kentwood knows each other – and their business – so the town backed her with loving support and encouragement during her local performances. Even now they welcome the pop star home with 'Welcome Home' signs. They even gave Kentwood the nickname 'Spears County'. In fact, Kentwood officials added a slogan to the town's welcome sign that says 'Home of Britney Spears'. Even though Britney has had a taste of the more glamorous cities such as London, New York and Paris, Kentwood has always been her home base, her retreat.

Winning first prize at talent shows and gaining the public exposure she craved was fairly easy on her own home turf. It propelled little Brinnie to continue her interests with enthusiasm, but she certainly wasn't without her obstacles, her disappointments. Britney will never forget the first time she auditioned for *The New Mickey Mouse Club* in 1990, when she was eight. Lynne was reading the newspaper one morning when her eyes fell on an announcement. The Disney variety show, which had originally aired in the 1950s, was making a big comeback and needed new 'Mouseketeers' to make up the cast for the new season. She mentioned the ad to Britney, and, not surprisingly, the eight-year-old was excited. She persuaded her mother to drive her to the audition in Atlanta, Georgia.

After putting on a near flawless performance, Britney was sure she'd get a spot on the show. The producers seemed to love her and she had given the audition everything she had. So it was to her surprise, and great disappointment, when she was deemed too young to join. This wouldn't be the first time in her career when age would play a factor: she would later be criticized as being too young to make a number one album.

Having faced rejection head on, Britney couldn't help but feel deflated and disappointed, so she reluctantly went back home to Kentwood with her mother. Refusing to let a setback get in her way, Britney vowed to keep trying.

She's never been a quitter; she's learned that life is a series of hurdles that need to be overcome.

She follows that philosophy still today. It also wasn't the last time Britney would have to face rejection. In fact, when Britney lost the Best New Artist Award to Christina Aguilera at the 2000 Grammys, she had her coping skills handy. This seasoned professional has had to keep a stiff upper lip on numerous occasions during her career, dispelling the myth that fame has been handed to her on a silver platter.

In front of her family, her friends, her peers, her critics, and, more dramatically, in front of the whole world, Britney handled the Grammy loss gracefully. She has said that she had just given a performance and was backstage when the winner was announced. Her first thought was that she had let down her family, along with all the other people on her team who support her; she knew how much everyone had hoped that she would receive the award. What eased the blow was that she focused on the positive: she had been nominated, and that was more than she had ever imagined. Any performer knows that rejection is part of the business and you can't let one loss stop you from persevering. Britney has said that her mother made her feel better with just the right words. She told her she loved her daughter no matter what.

After her first try at *The New Mickey Mouse Club,* Britney discovered that her audition was not entirely in vain. A producer from the show suggested that the Spears' contact an agent in New York who would be able to help their budding star, so they wasted little time getting on the phone to discuss Britney's future. Accompanied by her mother, who was pregnant with Jamie Lynn at the time, small-town Britney Spears flew to New York City to hone her skills. She took intensive dance classes at the Off-Broadway Dance Center and further explored her talents at Manhattan's Professional Performing Arts School (think of the movie *Fame* and you'll get an idea of the training

she received). In 1991, when she was nine, Britney performed in the Off-Broadway play *Ruthless*. The play, loosely based on the 1956 movie classic *The Bad Seed*, is about an evil little girl who will kill to get what she wants. The play never made it to Broadway, but many high schools have been putting it on because of its well-crafted script. Britney has said that it was fun to play a bad character.

During her stint in New York, Britney also starred in commercials for Mitsubishi and Malls Barbecue Sauce. When Jamie Lynn was born, the three lived together in a Manhattan sublet for a few months before returning home to the family. Britney's three summers in New York really opened her eyes.

For the first time she was independently pursuing her dreams in one of the biggest entertainment capitals of the world.

Instead of waking up to chirping birds as she had in rural Kentwood, Britney started her morning with the sound of honking cabs. Family friends back home raised their eyebrows at Britney's decision to take on the Big Apple, but Britney and her family knew that she had to take the chance if she was ever going to make her dreams come true.

A year later, in 1992, Britney won Miss Talent USA, winning a tiara, a four-foot trophy and $1,000. Later that year, Britney heard about auditions in Baton Rouge, Louisiana, to appear on *Star Search*, a nationally televised talent show. A number of today's artists had their starts on the talent show, which was popular in the late 1980s and early 1990s. Christina Aguilera and two of the members of Destiny's Child, Beyoncé and Kelly, had their first fifteen minutes of fame singing and dancing before the *Star Search* judges and audience.

Britney's audition impressed the producers and she was asked to perform on the show in Los Angeles in front of millions of TV viewers. She flew to Los Angeles, California, and won first prize that day. It was a great accomplishment because she was up against competition from around the country. Unfortunately, when she returned the following week she lost to another talented contestant, who is probably amazed at how far Britney has come since that competition.

Britney is glad she participated in so many performances during her childhood. She encourages other girls to pursue their goals and has said it's important to become good at your craft by taking part in as many events as possible. That's often how you stumble upon your big break.

For Britney, that memorable big break came when she was eleven and re-auditioned for *The New Mickey Mouse Club* against thousands of other hopeful kids from cities across the US and Canada. The producers remembered Britney from when she first auditioned two years earlier, and was deemed too young; they could see that she had grown up a lot and that her skills had been polished. This time she sealed the deal – and won her mouse ears – with a knockout performance. The wise Disney producers snatched the soon-to-be star and placed her alongside the other members of the cast, who were also brimming with talent.

Most Britney fans are well versed in these early years because this period is talked about so much in the press. It seems that every star today has had a start on *The New Mickey Mouse Club*. It was definitely an important moment in Britney history because the experience confirmed her decision, once and for all, that she was going to put her heart and soul into becoming a professional recording artist. It was a big moment for the Spears family, too: her mother moved with Britney and Jamie Lynn to Orlando, Florida, where the show was taped, with Brit's little sister. Britney's life-changing move would impact her career dramatically.

Britney bonded with her fellow Mouseketeers instantly because she was finally with kids her own age who loved to sing and dance the way she did. That famous cast included Christina Aguilera and Justin

Timberlake – who joined Britney as the youngest members of the cast – JC Chasez, Keri Russell (the future star of *Felicity*), the recording artist Tony Lucca and Nikki DeLoach, who would later join the group Innosense. There were others in the cast, who are currently carving out their own recording careers. It's not entirely far-fetched to imagine that yet another handful of former Mouseketeers will hit it big in the pop world, too.

Britney remembers every day of her stint in Orlando because it was such an exciting time. It was like living in Disney World. She shared a dressing room with Keri and remembers the curly-haired beauty, who was a few years older than Britney, playing with her sister Jamie Lynn. We can't forget that this was the time when Britney hung around with 'N Sync's JC Chasez and Justin Timberlake, way before they turned into the cool, successful guys they are today. In fact, they were still growing into their voices and acted like the young, adolescent boys they were. She remembers JC acting rambunctious and Justin following close behind his friend. *The New Mickey Mouse Club* proved to be a valuable training ground for Britney and a launching pad to great stardom – which was just around the corner.

Although it seems that most of today's pop stars have *The New Mickey Mouse Club* in their past, not all were on the variety show. In fact, Mandy Moore was a few years too young to try out since the show was discontinued in 1994 when she was ten, and Jessica Simpson auditioned but didn't make it on. Like Britney, Christina Aguilera was deemed too young when she first auditioned, at age nine, but she did get on the show later.

Stories in the media suggesting that Britney and Christina are feuding are untrue. Christina has said that the press has stirred up a rivalry but the fact is they are very different artists. She is proud of Britney for coming this far, and she knows Britney, even from the days

together on the show, as being a sweet girl. She has also remarked on her drive and stellar work ethics. Britney, in turn, has said Christina has what it takes: determination.

The two years on *The New Mickey Mouse Club* left Britney with wonderful memories.

As a first job it was better than paper delivery girl or bagger at the grocery store! She had the opportunity to sing and dance professionally on television with twenty other talented kids her age – and receive payment for what she loved.

The routine was simple. She would work for six months and then go back to Kentwood for the other six months to resume a normal life. Her day would start with a friendly wake-up call at 7 a.m. She'd have breakfast and than go to the school situated near the sound stage for classes that lasted until 12.30. After a quick lunch, the cast would rehearse all afternoon until four, then they'd tape the show for another three hours. The Mouseketeers would sing, dance, perform comedy skits and interview stars. Then the cast would eat dinner, complete their homework assignments and go to bed before starting another day of fun.

At the time, Britney thought her schedule was pretty full, but now when she looks back at those days she realizes she had it pretty good compared with the exhausting days she is experiencing now. To everyone's dismay, the show was called off in 1994, but those training years provided Britney with a strong work ethic and a clearer picture of where her future was headed. She said goodbye to her fellow Mouseketeers and returned to Kentwood to resume a normal life.

She had fun back with her classmates and even joined the basketball team – she was the point guard and her number was 9. Britney also attended homecoming, and basically did what every ninth-grader does, but really she missed her Orlando days and often wrote letters to her faraway cast mates. Little did she know that in just a few years she would reunite with her former Mouseketeers, joining

Justin and JC on tour and seeing Christina again at award shows. Britney was also poised to make a splash with a number one single, and, as if that were not enough icing on the cake, a number one album – but now we're getting ahead of our story.

Sensing his daughter's restlessness upon her return home, Jamie called up a contact he had in New York to see if Britney could get involved with other projects to keep her satisfied. They ended up talking with an entertainment lawyer named Larry Rudolph, who is a major force in the business and continues to manage Britney today along with her co-manager Johnny Wright. Rudolph knew Britney needed something big to cut her teeth on – she had already paid her showbiz dues with *Star Search, The New Mickey Mouse Club,* plays and commercials – so he asked her to put together a demo tape so he could pitch the budding star to record companies.

He told Britney's parents that it was the perfect time for her to break into the recording business because the new trend in music was leaning towards pop.

A new cycle was beginning and listeners wanted to return to feel-good music that you could sing and dance along to.

Rudolph pointed out that bands such as Backstreet Boys and 'N Sync, who were just beginning to really break through, were gaining immense popularity, due to their good looks, dynamic personalities and, most importantly, their pop sound. What was really lacking on the radio was a young female solo artist who represented the new sound of pop – a sound that could be described as a mix of traditional pop melodies with R&B harmonies and a slight rock edge. Basically, music was taking on the characteristics of many sounds and influences tied into one.

Rudolph stressed the importance of the demo tape, the ammunition he could fire at the big labels, so Britney made herself busy putting together a sample of her work. The key with a demo tape is to present yourself in a way that rings a bell with record executives: they want to be convinced that they're signing an artist who has that rare combination of talent mixed with far-reaching commercial appeal. Some stars have poured lots of money into producing slick, heavily produced demo tapes to edge out the competition. This doesn't always work to their benefit because it's far more important to convey your natural voice in its raw form. Relying simply on natural talent, Britney did just that and proved you don't need fancy technical work on your side if you have a naturally gifted voice. For this small-town girl, having the luxury of recording her songs in a professional sound studio was not an option, so she simply sang over an instrumental and sent Rudolph what she has called a 'dinky' one-song demo tape.

That tape proved to be more than 'dinky', because when it arrived at Jive Records, home of Backstreet Boys and most recently 'N Sync, and fell on the desk of Jeff Fenster, the senior vice-president of A&R (artists and repertoire), he loved it. He gave it a listen and was instantly impressed that Britney could convey emotional and commercial appeal. Put simply, she would be a hit with millions of people. And all it took was

her demo tape. It was that simple and it shows that, if you have a catchy voice, even a homemade tape will do the trick.

In June 1997, fifteen-year-old Britney was asked to fly to New York, where Jive's offices are located, and audition. In front of ten record executives, she had to prove that she could deliver in person. Obviously, Britney was under severe pressure – if she fluffed this big moment she might not get another chance, and she wasn't about to kiss her hopes of stardom goodbye. The label's president, Barry Weiss, has said that, when Britney first stood before the ten executives, she was nervous. That is, until she started to sing. Once she did and her professionalism kicked in, everyone was blown away.

Fast-forward to today, and it's a pretty safe assumption that Britney nailed her audition. When Britney was about to sing Whitney Houston's 'I Have Nothing', a song she loved by an artist she'd always admired, she was overwhelmed with pre-performance jitters. What some fans don't know is that Britney remembered a trick that has helped her get through some sticky situations. She simply blocked everyone out, closed her eyes and used all her concentration to focus on getting out that first note. The rest came easy.

Her performance was received with smiling faces, a round of applause and a development deal that turned into a fully-fledged solo recording contract.

This would be a remarkable accomplishment for any fifteen-year old, but for Britney it was just the beginning. What was about to happen would catapult her to dizzying heights of stardom. She was off to make her very first album.

Everything after that moved at lightning speed. Knowing he had finally found his female solo act amid an inundation of boy bands, Fenster worked at providing Britney with the best writers in the business. He called the writer/producer Max Martin, the prolific Swedish genius who has written songs for Backstreet Boys and 'N Sync, and told him about his find. In the spring of 1998, the then sixteen-year-old Britney boarded a plane to the Cheiron Studios in Stockholm, Sweden, where she met with Martin, who runs the outfit. After clicking so well musically with the hit master, she ended up recording much of her first album, as well as her second, in that tiny studio in Stockholm.

Max Martin is one of the most prolific forces in music today. The writer/producer has written some of the biggest hits of 2000, such as Backstreet Boys' 'I Want It That Way', 'N Sync's 'Bye Bye Bye' and of course Britney's '… Baby One More Time', as well as 'Crazy', 'Oops! … I Did It Again' and a string of other songs on Britney's albums.

Music insiders have often remarked on Martin's Midas touch: it seems that everything he touches goes gold – or, in Britney's case, platinum.

He simply knows how to work with artists to create fabulous songs. Britney agrees that Martin is a genius and has said that they have a special touch in Sweden. Having produced feel-good groups such as Abba and Ace of Base, Swedish writers and producers have proved they can produce music that people want to hear.

Although now Max Martin is a pop master, he used to be a heavy-metal singer for a group in Sweden called It's Alive. He has said that, even when he was thrashing and screaming in the loud band, he always had a way of writing tunes that had a pop feel. Even if that pop inclination didn't go far with his band, he has redirected his talents appropriately by writing for commercial artists. Now he runs Cheiron Studios, which is in fact not the flashy, glamorous building you would imagine but an unassuming cement-block structure sandwiched between two other nondescript buildings. Martin works hard with his team of producers, writers and musicians, spending long stretches of time working with the pop artists who fly in from the US. He is proud that fans have caught on to the fact that he works so closely with their idols. Knowing that 'N Sync, Backstreet Boys, Britney Spears and others record with Martin, fans have started to send him letters hoping he will pass them on to the designated artists. European fans stand outside the studio waiting eagerly for a glimpse of AJ from the Backstreet Boys, Lance from 'N Sync or the princess of pop, Britney Spears.

Although Martin worked with Britney on a lot of the songs on her albums, there are other talented writers and producers who also contributed their talents. For 'From the Bottom of My Broken Heart', 'Soda Pop' and 'E-mail My Heart', Britney worked with the writer/producer Eric Foster White, who has worked with Whitney Houston and Hi-Five. She spent hours recording with Foster in his New Jersey studio during the recording of … *Baby One More Time.* During breaks between songs, they would play darts together. For 'When Your Eyes Say It', Britney worked with Diane Warren, who is the queen of soaring ballads and has been writing for the last twenty years with some of the biggest names in music: Celine Dion, Aerosmith, 'N Sync, Christina Aguilera and countless others.

When she decided to include '(I Can't Get No) Satisfaction' on her second album, Britney knew she needed a fresh spin on the classic rock tune, so she turned to Rodney 'Darkchild' Jerkins, who co-wrote Brandy and Monica's duet 'The Boy is Mine'. He's also worked with Jennifer Lopez, Will Smith, Whitney Houston, Puff Daddy and, most recently, Michael Jackson. The result? A slower version with Britney's sassy signature style. Britney looked within for 'Dear Diary', the confessional ballad that she co-wrote. Listening to

the song is like tearing out an entry from her diary: it really lets you in on her private world.

What happens in the studio is always a mystery to us, as well as the artist. It usually takes hours of talking, writing and working out the kinks to get a song perfect. There can be days when the artist and producer work laboriously on finding the right sound, and then there are times when the song is completed within an hour.

After Britney's full-fledged promotional tour, during which she met DJs at radio stations across the country, talked with new fans after her mall performances and talked with editors at teen magazines, she waited anxiously for her single to be released. In October 1999, '... Baby One More Time' was presented to the world and she got busy working on the video that is now an MTV classic. Britney's story proves that perseverance, hard work and some luck thrown into the mix create a recipe for success.

Britney has said that, at the time she was promoting her first album, she was so new to the business that everything felt like one big blur. Decisions affecting her career were being made left and right, and during the initial stages Britney was shy about voicing opinions. There was so much to think about. Who would be her choreographer? Who would direct her video? How would it look? She would often hold in her feelings because she wasn't experienced with different situations and wouldn't know what to say. As time went on, she grew more confident and clear-headed about the direction she wanted to go in. She admits that she would often wait until the last minute to say something and then it would be too late and she'd blow up. Those feelings are universal, and easy to empathize with. Now, she's gained so much experience that she feels much more self-assured and expressive about the creative decisions that have to be made on a daily basis: Britney has the final say with everything she does, whether it's her selection of songs, the look and treatment for her videos or even the design of her album cover.

She admitted a year after it was released that she wasn't crazy about the photo on ... Baby One More Time because it was out of date from the beginning. The cute photo featuring a smiling Britney dressed in a red shirt, blue miniskirt and platform sandals was taken during a promotional photo shoot when she was fifteen. When the album was released, Britney had just turned seventeen, so she looked

much older than the photo on the album cover. Having learned from that, she was adamant about getting an accurate look for the cover of *Oops! ... I Did It Again.* She was a perfectionist about finding the right fashion, hair and make-up stylists, who would understand her vision. After all, millions of people now own the CD and look at the photo, so it only makes sense that she would strive for an album cover representative of her current image.

Britney's involvement in her work has been to her benefit because, as history has shown, some new artists fall prey to dishonest people who make the wrong decisions for them. For instance, there have been many VH1 television specials about teen stars from the past who made bad business decisions, were ill-treated by their handlers, and sadly lost all control of their career. Today, artists have learned from their predecessors' mistakes and are therefore much more savvy when it comes to their contracts and other paperwork that trail their every step.

Britney is one of those artists who pay close attention to every detail of their careers.

She makes sure she always surrounds herself with good, trustworthy people who keep her interests a priority.

For the fans who have closely followed Britney's every move since she became the new artist to watch in late 1998, it's obvious how much she has changed. Although she's still the warm-hearted family girl who likes to have fun, she has also come into her own as a strong person, one who takes her work seriously. She has said that she doesn't just want to be known as a teen who likes to sing, dance and swoon for movie stars: she wants her fans to know that below her bubbly exterior is a hard-working girl who is devoted to living her dream, inspiring others to do the same, and putting out music her fans will enjoy.

Remarkably, Britney's gone from a shy, unknown kid from Louisiana to a multi-platinum-selling personality – and she's done her growing up in the watchful public eye. Compare the photo on her debut cover, *... Baby One More Time* with the one on her second album *Oops! ... I Did It Again* to see how she's grown up. Sure, she's dyed her hair and experimented with different fashion looks and make-up styles, but what's really different about Britney today is that she's matured musically and personally. She's playing a bigger role in the music she sings and she's showing a healthy supply of confidence. You can see it in her eyes, this girl is happy with herself.

What makes a hit album?

It was easy for us to pick up our first Britney album, slip it into the CD player, and listen to it for hours, but what actually went into making the smash-hit album? Well, Britney had to learn the songs, listen to the demo tape, record it, think of video ideas, promote it, and then wait for the results from the chart shows to see how her music was rating with her fans and the critics. Max Martin had originally written the song '… Baby One More Time' for the R&B trio TLC, but their record label thought it would be better for Five. Martin then decided to take it to Britney so she could sing it, and the rest, as they say, is history.

For her second album, Britney has said that it was easier because she was more experienced, but she did have the added pressure to be a number one artist all over again. To confirm her musical credibility with critics, she included more ballads, such as 'Don't Let Me Be the Last To Know'.

She also wanted her music to reflect her current mood, so she aimed at making it edgier and funkier.

For songs like 'Oops! … I Did It Again' and 'Lucky', she teamed up with Max Martin in Sweden again. *Oops!* sold 1,319 million copies in the first week, so she's clearly found the sound people want to hear!

Britney also recorded in Geneva, Switzerland, with Shania Twain's husband Mutt Lange for 'Don't Let Me Be the Last To Know' and in New York with Rodney Jerkins. She had chatted with Jerkins about collaborating on the album when she was backstage at the 1999 Grammy Award nominations. He told her he wanted to give her a sassier sound, like Janet Jackson's. That, of course, was music to Britney's ears because Janet has been her idol since she started listening to her funky tunes as a kid. Ultimately, Rodney would redo Britney's version of '(I Can't Get No) Satisfaction'.

Ten things you didn't know about Britney

(1) Her album *Oops! … I Did It Again* was originally going to be titled *Sunflower*.

(2) As everyone knows, she clicked with England's Prince William over email. But what some don't know is that she has English blood in her. Her mother's family still live in parts of England.

(3) Like other high-profile stars, Britney has tried to disguise herself with different props so she isn't recognized in public. One time she wore a long black wig (think Cher's hair) at the urging of her dancers. Unfortunately, her disguise didn't work. People noticed her even more than if she had just put on a baseball cap. She has said that it's getting progressively more difficult to go out in public without getting mobbed

(4) When she came to New York to start working on her debut album *… Baby One More Time*, her record company, Jive, put her up in an apartment with Fee Culotta. This was her home away from home while she started recording her first album.

(5) On 2 December 1998, she celebrated her seventeenth birthday on the tour bus during her opening stint for 'N Sync's tour. Justin, Lance, Joey and Chris sang her a harmonized version of 'Happy Birthday'. She celebrated her eighteenth birthday by singing 'Silent Night' at the Christmas lighting at New York's

Rockefeller Center. Then she headed to the trendy, red-velvet-roped Greenwich Village club, Halo, surrounded by family and friends, including 'N Sync. Every year the public celebrate another year for Britney, wondering what she'll surprise us with next. She was presented with a diamond necklace from Jive Records to commemorate 10 million copies sold of ... *Baby One More Time.*

6 One of Britney's most treasured recordings is the song '(I Can't Get No) Satisfaction', which was originally a 1965 hit for the Rolling Stones. Mick Jagger, the lead singer of the group, rarely allows other artists to cover his tunes, but he granted Britney's wish. The reason the song is special for her is that, when her friend first got a car, the two would drive around happily singing 'Satisfaction'. At first people told her not to cover the classic rock number, but she recorded it anyway. She purposely made it different with the help of the producer Rodney Jerkins, so the songs wouldn't be compared to each other. She says she would also like to cover Prince's 1984 hit 'Purple Rain'.

7 Britney's bodyguard, Big Rob (Robert Feggans), takes his job seriously so Britney feels secure. The 350-pound guy benches 380, so he's in top form to watch over Britney's safety. One time, Britney was on a hotel balcony talking privately with her mother when a strange guy leaned over his own balcony and began to take rather too much interest in their conversation. In no time, Big Rob was to the rescue.

8 The residents of Kentwood have created a museum for their famous hometown girl at the request of fans. It's slated to open in 2001. That's right, Britney will have her own museum, which will be a part of the already existing Kentwood Museum. There will be a gift shop and Britney memorabilia. Lynne and Jamie Spears have donated items, such as the necklace she wore at the Mardi Gras parade and the two dresses she wore for her performances on *Star Search.*

9 After picking family and friends first, Britney says the next person she would like to spend the day with is the US talk-show queen Oprah Winfrey because Britney finds her incredibly interesting.

10 When Britney found out she broke records with her first week's sales of *Oops! ... I Did It Again*, she was in a studio in Orlando, Florida, rehearsing for her summer tour. Always the hard worker, Britney took a minute's break to hug her manager Johnny Wright and toasted the triumphant feat with a glass of Coca-Cola. Then she got right back to rehearsing.

chapter four

Dear Diary: Her Private Life

Most of the world knows Britney's public persona, the singing, dancing star who smiles brightly for the camera. She radiates a larger-than-life image, one who always seems energetic and on. Britney down? Never, or at least that is how it seems. Remarkably, Britney puts on a brave face even when up against challenges; she is a trooper who puts her fans before herself. Britney is human, however, and well hidden from the public eye is her deeply private side, which she reveals only to those close to her, such as family and friends.

What is this pop princess really like when she's not decked from head to toe in dressy duds, eye-grabbing make-up and perfect hair? As she writes in her confessional song 'Dear Diary', she's an emotional person with deep feelings just like any girl on the planet. She's just like you and me – a human being who likes to enjoy the good things in life.

Britney loves to eat cookie-dough ice cream from the carton, hang out in her night things all day and take long, relaxing bubblebaths.

In fact, when she's at award shows and people ask her to hang out and go to one party after the next, she bows out gracefully because, she has said, she's not a party animal. She'd much rather have a hot bath and a good night's sleep. Britney's also a girl with a great imagination, so, when she has the downtime to think about things other than scheduled interviews, touring and recording, she takes full advantage and dreams about things that make her happy.

One subject that Britney could spend lots of time dreaming about is love. Like many girls, she hopes that one day she'll meet Mr Right, her perfect soul mate, who will sweep her off her feet and take her to a land where she can live happily ever after. In fact, she went to a fortune teller just for fun and was told that she will marry a guy with dark hair when she's 23. She has dreams of living in a beautiful house with a husband and three kids somewhere close to her family in Kentwood. Early marriages run in her family: her brother Bryan, four years older than she, has (at the time of writing) a fiancée, Blaize, and her parents married in

their early twenties. On the topic of marriage, Britney has said that her tastes in guys change as frequently as her tastes in clothes, so she doesn't understand why people marry so young.

Now that Britney is in the limelight, everyone wants to know about her love life, especially sensationalist tabloids. What often happens is that stories get blown out of proportion and Britney is falsely linked with a list of eligible guys. The truth is, Britney has her crushes and, if time permits, she does try to go on the occasional date, but being a pop star isn't always as glamorous as the gossip columns portray it. Britney has said that when she reads the gossip, that she's going out with this guy and that guy, she laughs and thinks, I wish.

One persistent story that won't go away is the one about Britney and Justin Timberlake being in a serious relationship. Gallons of ink have been shed on the subject and it has meant that Britney's personal life has unfairly met intense public scrutiny. Britney has admitted that she and Justin are good friends and enjoy each other's company – and sometimes kiss – but that it is nothing serious. It's understandable why the stories surface: Britney and Justin have been friends since they were eleven on *The New Mickey Mouse Club*. Plus, they've toured together and their paths often cross just because they're in the same business. In reality, however, both Britney and Justin have been working at high speeds to promote their new albums and embark on non-stop tours. What that means is lots of flying around the world, sometimes on a weekly basis with hardly enough time to sleep, let alone maintain a serious relationship. So, it only makes sense to take Britney at her word. She has said she adores Justin, and vice versa, but sometimes a friendship really is just a friendship. Time will tell.

Another bit of juicy hearsay off the grapevine is that Britney is dating the blond Prince William, the first born son of the late Princess Diana, and the heir to the English throne. Although such majestic talk is flattering – Britney confesses she'd love to be dating the Prince – she insists this tall tale is yet another false bit of fodder created by the gossip hounds. The real story is that Britney's record company sent the Prince an autographed photo of Britney when they learned that he's a big fan of her music. He sent a handwritten letter of thanks, which started a brief correspondence of emails between the Prince and Britney. Again, in reality, having Prince William as a casual cyber-

pal certainly doesn't amount to a royal wedding in Britney's near future.

There was also speculation that Britney was dating Robbie Carrico, from the pop group Boyz 'N Girlz United, because the friends have attended events together, like the movie premiere for the teen romance *Drive Me Crazy*, which starred Melissa Joan Hart and Adrian Grenier. Robbie and Britney also hung out together at Britney's eighteenth birthday party, but again they are just friends.

The movie was originally titled *Next to You*, but it was renamed after a remix of Britney's song '(You Drive Me) Crazy' became the featured song on the soundtrack. Britney worked with Melissa on promoting it and they became good friends in the process. The success of *Drive Me Crazy* caused a resurgence in sales of Britney's album, confirming that she has longevity with her music.

So how does Britney deal with all this media matchmaking?

Her charm is that she knows how to roll her eyes, shrug her shoulders and just say 'whatever' when dogged with controversies.

She has said that, when she first had to deal with the relentless gossip that seems to pop up in the press daily, she felt overwhelmed. It was like that bad feeling you get in school when you're being picked on. To make matters worse, Britney was being subjected to all this tittle-tattle in front of the whole world. She admits that being a teenager comes with extra worries and that it's a time when you're extra vulnerable, so gossip can be hard to handle.

Britney has also found that the tabloids treat her unfairly because she's new to the business and they like to drum up stories of competition and feuding. On the topic of Christina Aguilera, Britney has said that they are friends but they don't always get to see each other because their careers keep them busy. The former Mouseketeers hang out whenever their paths cross – at award shows, for instance. When stories spread that the two artists are enemies, Britney has to roll her eyes again. She complains that Mariah and Madonna are never compared to each other as she and Christina are, and she has said it's because she and Christina are both young. Britney would rather spend her time and energy on making music and meeting her fans than learning to keep the paparazzi at bay.

One topic Britney is always happy to discuss is her fixation with the top leading actors of the day. Did anyone say Brad Pitt and Ben Affleck? If Britney could pick a dream date to have dinner with she has said it would be Pitt. After all, she's already had her meeting with Ben Affleck, which, of course, became a story blown out of proportion in the gossip columns.

The real story is that Britney was doing an interview for E! (Entertainment) television and casually mentioned she thought Affleck was cute. Ben was going through his on/off relationship with Gwyneth Paltrow and at the time it was off, so Britney jokingly looked into the camera and sent a personal wish to

Ben that if he was watching she wanted him to know she'd date him in a second. Because of the chatty nature of showbiz, information gets passed around quickly. After Britney made that remark on national television, Ben's publicist heard about it and called Britney's publicist to arrange for Britney and Ben to meet.

They met for dinner at Planet Hollywood in Los Angeles, and, funnily enough, each star brought along a friend to diffuse the tension. Britney remembers feeling secretly very nervous, but she purposely tried to appear outwardly cool in front of her crush. Before meeting him, she has said that she spent 45 minutes trying to decide what to wear.

At the time, Ben was working on a movie about the music business and wanted Britney's take, so the two had lots to talk about. Britney was more than happy to share her thoughts on everything she'd learned so far from her own career, and Ben was more than happy to listen.

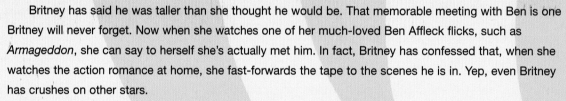

One of the weirdest feelings in the world is to actually meet a famous person you know only from the movies. It's even stranger when that person happens to be your crush.

Britney has said he was taller than she thought he would be. That memorable meeting with Ben is one Britney will never forget. Now when she watches one of her much-loved Ben Affleck flicks, such as *Armageddon*, she can say to herself she's actually met him. In fact, Britney has confessed that, when she watches the action romance at home, she fast-forwards the tape to the scenes he is in. Yep, even Britney has crushes on other stars.

In her hit song 'Oops! ... I Did It Again', Britney sings about a girl who flirts with a guy she isn't that serious about. Britney has said that she's the opposite of that fictional character, and, in her experiences, she's usually the one who gets hurt. Even though she appears carefree and confident on stage, she's surprisingly shy when it comes to love. While some girls are chatty with guys, Britney has said that she often gets speechless around a sweetie she has eyes for. It doesn't help that guys are often intimidated by her because she's famous, so if she's at a party she's rarely approached directly by an admirer.

Britney's very first love was Reggie Jones, whom she dated back in Kentwood. As the story goes, Reggie was a friend of Britney's brother, Bryan, and, as he spent more and more time at the Spears' house, he began to develop a crush on Britney. One day, he asked Jamie and Lynne if he could take Britney to a dance. They permitted it and Britney and Reggie started a relationship that lasted for two years, up until Britney recorded ... *Baby One More Time.* It was at that time that life took a dramatic turn: Britney's schedule stepped up to a hectic pace that made maintaining a relationship difficult. Flying from one country to the next meant the relationship had to be long-distance – and that can leave little room for quality time.

So what really happened between the childhood lovebirds? Britney has said that they simply grew apart. She has admitted that she doesn't know if she'll ever love someone as much as she loved her first boyfriend, but that remains to be seen. Reggie has said that their relationship was a special time he'll never forget and that he wishes her happiness and success. Reggie and Britney no longer talk.

Britney agrees that being in love is fantastic – after all, most of her songs are about that very topic – and that it's a feeling not unlike the one she gets when she's performing on stage. She's also said, however, that, because her crazy schedule leaves little room for a boyfriend, she's come to accept that it can be OK to be single because she knows she can survive without a boyfriend. Of course, if fate meant her to meet someone special, she'd be thrilled.

Although Britney plays a sassy school cheerleader in her video for '… Baby One More Time', that doesn't mean she was the popular girl at school growing up. She has said that she had lots of different types of friends, but that she wasn't the girl all the guys went for.

If Britney was going to go on a perfect date, what would it be like? Well, there'd have to be some slow dancing to songs like Eric Clapton's 'Wonderful Tonight', because she loves that romantic track. Then, she'd like the guy to dedicate a song to her, such as Van Morrison's 'Brown Eyed Girl', because that's a song she loves to fast-dance to. She has also said that a romantic dinner at a nice restaurant and a movie would complete her perfect night out with someone special.

Do you have a boyfriend? This is a question Britney is repeatedly asked and she often responds that she's too busy for a serious relationship. Still, the question keeps getting asked. She has recently said that she hopes to have more time for a personal life this year when she gets a break from the all-consuming demands of touring and recording.

When that perfect guy does come around, what is Britney hoping for? She has said that she likes a guy with confidence, someone who is comfortable and happy with himself. She also looks for a sense of fun, so serious guys need not apply. She also wants someone she can talk to for hours, someone who will be her best friend. Most importantly, the top qualities she looks for are trust and honesty, because in love those are the foundations that are crucial to a relationship. Although she's a romantic and would love a guy to surprise her with a homemade candlelit dinner, she especially likes a sensitive sweetie who will express his true feelings to her without resorting to game playing.

What's your star sign? This is a question Britney likes to ask because she admits she likes to follow astrology and learn about people's different cosmic characteristics. And she knows that astrologers often pair her sign, Sagittarius, with Leo, Gemini and Aries. Sagittarians are known to love their freedom, so they are good matches with independent signs who also like lots of space. This goal-oriented Sagittarian gets along well with guys who have their own set of dreams and won't stifle her or step on her toes. She does feel strongly about commitment, and she has said that, if her boyfriend made eyes at another girl and started to flirt, she'd first try to control her jealousy and wait to see what happened. If the flirting continued, she'd ditch the guy fast and find someone who was worth her time.

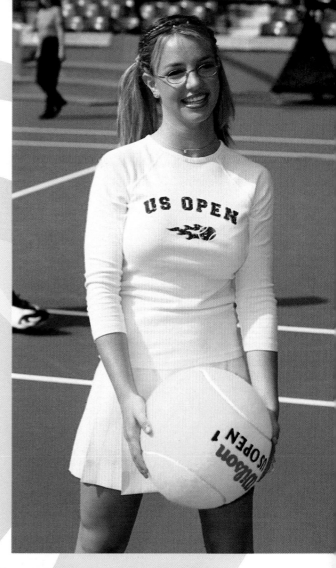

Her advice for other girls is to always be yourself because then the guy will get to know the real you and like you for your unique qualities.

She also insists that it's important to be natural – skip the heavy make-up and flashy clothes – because nothing makes a relationship work more than pure chemistry. Finally, have fun and don't worry too much about every detail.

Fame has also made her more selective when picking the right guy because she wants someone who's interested in her, not the fame. She admits it would be easier to date a guy in the music business because he'd have a better understanding of her busy schedule and the demands she has to meet every day. Britney is a self-confessed romantic, and she has said that if she fell in love with someone outside the business, such as a guy working at McDonald's, she'd have to follow her heart.

If you listen to the words she's singing in songs such as 'Sometimes', 'Can't Make You

Love Me' and 'When Your Eyes Say It', you'll catch a glimpse of what matters to Britney. 'Should I tell him how I feel or would that scare him away?' writes Britney in her self-penned ballad 'Dear Diary'.

Britney's best friends

Britney makes a point of including her best friends in her busy life whenever she can so, when she was arranging her trip to Hawaii for her concert in Waikiki, she asked her friends Courtney and Jansen and her cousin Laura Lynne to come along. When they're on the road with her, she brings her buds to her fave places, like Virgil's, a New York City restaurant that serves up delicious Southern cooking. Britney has grown up with these girls and they're close. It can be difficult to leave your friends behind even for a little while, so, when Britney landed her record deal and moved away from home, she had to adjust to long-distance friendships. She's still in touch with about six close buds from her childhood and emails them when she's on the road.

Going to school at Park Lane Academy, Britney made friends with all types of people instead of sticking to one clique. Britney takes her friendships seriously and has said that she looks for friends who are trustworthy and honest.

She appreciates her friends keeping her in line and doesn't want them to kiss up to her.

When she gets home to Kentwood, she calls up her six close buds to go shopping or see a movie.

One of Britney's closest friends is her cousin Laura Lynne Covington. They would play together growing up and, even when Britney is on the road, they call each other constantly and talk about all their life issues.

When Britney gets to go home every six weeks, her friends always let her be herself, she says, and when they catch up after a long time apart they never talk about the music business. Instead, Britney likes to hear about what's been happening in her friends' lives. She admits that most of her friends have boyfriends, so it's getting harder to reserve girl time without the guys interfering.

Quiz : Would you and Britney be friends?

1) If Britney called you on a boring, rainy Saturday afternoon the very first thing she would suggest you do is go
- **a.** shopping
- **b.** to the movies
- **c.** golfing

2) When Britney is really tired and stressed out, you know that she likes to treat herself to a
- **a.** bubblebath
- **b.** party
- **c.** workout at the gym

3) If you were in the bookstore with Britney, she'd probably take you to
- **a.** the romance aisle
- **b.** the science-fiction aisle
- **c.** the finance aisle

4) If there's one piece of gossip you know Britney doesn't mind all that much it's
- **a.** her supposed romance with Prince William
- **b.** her supposed lip-syncing
- **c.** her supposed plastic surgery

5) Without having to ask her, you already know her astrological sign is
- **a.** Sagittarius
- **b.** Scorpio
- **c.** Capricorn

6) Of the following, Britney would choose
- **a.** baby blue
- **b.** powder pink
- **c.** forest green

7) Britney's first true love would be
- **a.** Reggie Jones
- **b.** Ben Affleck
- **c.** Prince William

8) If Britney took you to New York and said she wanted you to try a restaurant known for its delicious Southern cooking, she'd take you to
- **a.** Virgil's
- **b.** Lola's
- **c.** Jezebel's

9) If you could surprise Britney with an energy-blasting drink during one of her video shoots, you would arrive on the set with a
- **a.** mochaccino
- **b.** Gatorade
- **c.** Coke

10) If you were with Britney backstage at one of her concerts and she was about to go on stage, she would ask you to join her and the dancers for
- **a.** a prayer
- **b.** a game of hackey-sack
- **c.** a massage

How did you score?

If you scored mostly As you're **Britney's friend forever.** You know Britney so well, you could surprise her with a birthday gift and she'd like it instantly. You know she loves to shop and that she adores blue. You're a good friend who wouldn't bum her out by bringing up gossip about her – although you know she gets a kick out of the Prince William story. If she was having an exhausting day of work, you'd cheer her up with her fave energy-boosting drink, a mochaccino. You click so well with Britney.

If you scored mostly Bs, then you're **Britney's bum-around bud.** You're a good friend who always remembers Britney's birthday, although you may not know her star sign right away. You know she likes pastels, but you're torn about whether she prefers, let's say, pink or blue. You know how much Britney loves Southern food (after all, her mother makes a mean chicken dumpling dish) and that she hates scandal-mongering (you're not totally up on all the gossip that surrounds your friend Britney because that's not what's important to you). You may not know Britney inside and out, but you stick by her no matter what, and she cherishes your friendship.

So what if you scored mostly Cs? Well, then you'd be **Britney's casual chum.** You're a cool acquaintance of Britney's, but there are probably things about her that you just don't know. You'd have a blast together backstage, but, if she started making a circle with her dancers, you might think she's going to start a game of hackey-sack when really she's praying. You would support Britney in her dreams, but you may not know that the one thing she really likes when she's stressed is a bubblebath. Instead, you would probably bring her to a party to help her chill out. In any case, the details don't matter because you could grow to be super-close pals.

Brit's vocabulary

This Southern girl has her own cool words and phrases. Check them out:

Lockdown: This is when Britney is with a make-up artist getting done up, and listening to her fave CDs before a show, such as Janet Jackson's 1989 *Rhythm Nation* or 1997's *Velvet Rope.*

She's down home: This is what Britney calls a cool girl in the business who doesn't have an ego and who keeps it real.

Crazy: A word Britney uses hundreds of times a day.

Whatever: Her response for when the gossip gets out of control.

Such a goob: goofball.

How cool is this?: When she's amazed by something.

I can't complain: Even though she gets little sleep and lives a busy life, she refuses to complain because she's happy living her dream.

Gosh, yes: This explains itself!

Vibed off me: When an audience picks up on Britney's enthusiasm during a show.

Hit me one more time: Give me a signal.

And Britney's fave phrase? 'Live each day to the fullest as if it were your last.'

Mama's Girl

Chapter five

When Britney won the Favorite New Pop-Rock Artist award at the 1999 American Music Awards, who did she call first on her cell phone? When she's sitting on the tour bus looking through the window and feeling lonely, who does she feel like talking to? When she's upset about another false story about her in the tabloids, who does she turn to first? The answer to all those questions has to be her mother, Lynne, because she knows that there's no one else in the world who knows her more.

Britney has said that whenever she reads yet another story in the press which make her cry, she'll telephone her mother straight away. With just the right words, Lynne will help her distraught daughter deal with the crisis. She has said that it's her mother who taught her to just say 'OK, whatever' to the gossip. She's also learned how to ignore the negative press and to focus on herself. Having learned from her mother, Britney advises other girls to pay attention to themselves and who they are, instead of letting outside influences interfere with their personal growth and happiness.

Britney's mother provides a comfort zone that makes her feel happy no matter how bad her day has been.

When she's homesick, she just has to hear her mother's warm voice and she's at ease. When she's eating bought food on the road she remembers her mother's delicious cooking.

As we've seen, Britney insists on coming home every six weeks, and, when she does finally step through the door of her home, she goes right to her bed and sleeps, usually till noon or later. After she has arrived, a mother-daughter ritual is to turn off the phones, catch up on the latest news together, share a pint of strawberry ice cream with cool whip, and nap. They enjoy spending quality time together and go shopping and get their nails done. Another ritual is to watch movies together in the living room. Lynne, Britney and Jamie Lynn will change for bed, drag their blankets and pillows into the living room, and snuggle together watching their fave flicks, such as *Breakfast at Tiffany's* or *Armageddon*.

Lynne makes the dishes she knows Britney adores – grits, for instance, or chicken dumplings and grilled cheese. Britney especially enjoys summer in Kentwood because it's crawfish season and her mother prepares it just the way Britney likes.

Britney admits that it can be weird to be away from home and then come back to rules, but she has

always respected her mother's wishes. If her mother asks her to be home by 11.30, she listens. Although Britney has her own room, she prefers to sleep next to her mother for comfort when she's back home.

Like mother like daughter, as the saying goes, and Britney is very much her mother's baby. She admits that her mother is her best friend and that she's a lot like her in good ways and bad. Although she bites her nails and worries like her mother, Britney has also learned how to remain positive even if life throws you a curve ball. Britney also looks a lot like her mother and inherited Lynne's big brown eyes and wide smile. She has said that her mother glows when she walks into a room, and she has always wanted to grow up to be just like her.

Whenever there is a big music event, Britney asks her record company if she can bring her mother along, as she did for the 2000 Grammy Awards. In Lynne's journal, which she posts on the web for fans to read, she wrote that they went to a pre-Grammy party together and spent the evening meeting a host of stars. They left the party at a reasonable time, however, because Britney had to wake up early the next morning for a run-through of her Grammy performance the next day.

They sat together in the fourth row at the Grammys in front of Kid Rock. When Britney lost the Best New Artist Award to Christina Aguilera, Lynne told Britney, 'Always be thankful for what you have. No one can win everything.' The next day they forgot all about the loss by cooking up a bunch of Britney's fave dishes, such as chicken dumplings and scalloped potatoes.

Another fun trip for Lynne was when Britney performed her huge, televised concert in the spring of 2000 in Hawaii. She thought it would be fun for her mother to come along and enjoy the breathtaking vistas. Lynne wrote on her web journal that Hawaii was paradise.

Way before she was dominating the *Billboard* charts, *TRL* and award shows, Britney remembers that it was her mother who helped her reach her dreams. It was Britney's mother who first noticed her daughter's raw talents. Lynne remembers that Britney had a knack for holding notes and hitting the right key. Lynne also remembers listening to Britney sing on the trampoline and when she was a little baby.

When she wanted to go to gymnastics class, Britney remembers her mother driving her over one hour each way so she could get the training she wanted. They would sing along in the car to groups such as Journey. In fact, Britney included Journey's song 'Open Arms' on her latest tour

and, when her mother heard it while sitting in the audience, she cried.

When she landed a spot on *The New Mickey Mouse Club*, Britney had to move to Orlando, Florida, where the show was taped, so her mother kept her company with her younger sister Jamie Lynn. And, while there are 'stage mothers' who push their kids to be stars, Britney has always said that her mother would have been happy to have just cooked for and watched over her daughter, but, because Britney showed a passion for performing from the start, Lynne encouraged her.

Britney wanted to find a special way to show her mother how thankful she is for her support and love, so she surprised her with a generous gift that will last a lifetime. She got her mother a new house. It's always been Lynne's dream to move out of the three-bedroom ranch that the family have squeezed into all these years, and move into a more spacious home. Britney is helping her mother's dream come true by hiring contractors to build the Spears family a bigger house on a bigger plot in another section of Kentwood. The house is everything Lynne hoped for: it's built in the Tudor style, with three fireplaces that you can light with a remote control, a luxury device made famous in the movie *Clueless*.

Britney's close relationship with her mother has helped the famous performer stay grounded.

She knows that, if she lets anything get to her head, her mother will keep her in line. That goes for everyone in Britney's family. She remembers pestering her brother by singing and dancing to Madonna songs when they were growing up. When Bryan told Britney to be quiet because he was trying to watch television, she would just roll her eyes at him. That bantering is typical of sibling relationships and Britney wouldn't have it any other way.

Bryan always makes an effort to stop by the house for dinner so he can catch up with his younger sister. Britney also makes a special effort to attend her younger sister's softball games because she knows how important it is to have your family around you during a winning point. Britney used to play too – she was a pitcher – and so she gives Jamie Lynn first-hand advice. When Britney was planning to shoot the video for 'Lucky', she rearranged the plans in order to get the video completed in two days instead of three so she could attend her sister's dance recital. Some music insiders have remarked on the close resemblance between Britney and her kid sis, and some wonder if Jamie Lynn would ever pursue a career in music. For now, Jamie Lynn is happy to focus on sports, according to Britney.

Britney adores her younger sister and has called her a spitfire who has an abundance of confidence. She has said that Jamie Lynn likes to sing along to her songs and even challenges her older sister with singing competitions in the house. For an especially memorable bonding event, Britney joined her family at the Mardi Gras parade, where she served as grand marshal. She spent four hours amid 28 floats, 42 marching bands and thousands of parade-goers.

Video Magic

It's impossible to think of Britney Spears without picturing her visually fantastic videos. She has catapulted herself – high kicks and all – into our homes with jaw-dropping, tear-shedding, smile-inducing abandon. When it comes to videos, Britney's got it. When she pops up on MTV or on *The Box*, the instant reaction is to reach for the remote and up the volume. And that's even after several hundred viewings. In fact, even though MTV has to 'retire' videos after they appear 65 times, fans still request Britney's recordings months after they're released.

Fans say they can't get enough of Britney's slick, sparkling, engrossing videos because they're entertaining, like watching a movie.

That's the same feeling Britney experienced when she first saw Michael Jackson's video for 'Thriller', and she hopes to use that inspiration to create videos others will love for years to come. She has said that she insists on producing well-thought-out videos because, once they appear on MTV and the whole world sees them, they're in people's memories for good. If they're not perfect, that's something Britney can't live with.

When it's announced that Britney is stopping by MTV's *Total Request Live* headquarters, situated right in the middle of New York's bustling Times Square where yellow cabs and crowds of people pack the area, fans line up in front of the big window facing Broadway holding homemade signs pledging their fan loyalty. They're hoping to catch a glimpse of Britney announcing the video countdown with *TRL*'s host Carson Daly in the glass-encased studio. Sometimes, a fan from the crowd is picked to go up to the studio to meet Britney personally.

What makes a Britney video so compelling changes from one clip to the next. With Britney's video debut '... Baby One More Time', which first appeared on *TRL* in November 1999, fans say the schoolroom setting and spirited attitude caught their eye. But what really inspired them to request the video over and over was Britney's dancing.

'... Baby One More Time' was supposed to be an entirely different video than we see now. The first treatment presented to Britney was an animated video featuring Power Ranger-type characters. Britney

thought the concept was too juvenile: she wanted her debut video to be edgy and daring. One day, while sitting on a plane, Britney had a brainwave that would solve all the problems with her video. She visualized a school setting with lots of dancing, so she told her record company about it and they phoned the British director Nigel Dick, who is known for his cutting-edge creations. He was already experienced with pop music, having directed Backstreet Boys' video for 'As Long As You Love Me'. Britney also had a say in the casting. She asked her cousin Chad, who was working as a model for Abercrombie & Fitch, to play the love interest, and she asked her chaperone Fee to play the teacher. For two days the crew worked feverishly getting the shots perfect at Rydell High School in Venice, California, where the movie Grease was filmed. As is typical of video shoots, there was lots of downtime, so the girls on the set played cards and board games while the guys kicked around a soccer ball. All the hard work paid off because the video turned out to be one of the most requested on MTV.

Britney's second video, for 'Sometimes', didn't run as smoothly. Britney's notorious knee accident came at the worst time, just as she was in the middle of rehearsing her dance steps for 'Sometimes'. It was February of 1999, a month after her album went number one and her life started getting crazy, when Britney was in a Los Angeles studio doing a step that required her to lift her leg high in the air. As she did, her standing leg buckled and she badly twisted her knee. When she first went to the doctor to check on the seriousness of her accident, she was told it would be fine with the help of a physiotherapist. But, when the pain persisted after a few days, she went to a specialist doctor at the New Orleans Doctors' Hospital who had to remove the torn cartilage. When the doctor told her she needed surgery she remembers bursting into tears.

Unfortunate mishaps never come at a good time, but this accident hit Britney just as she was in the middle of a high-powered month of activities. She was scheduled to finish her video, attend the Forty-first Annual Grammy Awards, and kick off a promotional tour throughout Britain, but her plans were changed so she could recover for the designated six weeks. Britney has said that it was a terrible time because she's such an energetic person and hated having to be in a wheelchair and on crutches when she really wanted to be dancing.

Fortunately, the video turned out to be a success, although the

ballad didn't climb the charts as high as her debut. 'Sometimes' was shot in Malibu, California, at the beach, but ironically the weather was freezing. Britney mustered up her acting skills to make it look convincingly warm and pleasant. The video, directed again by the trendy British director Nigel Dick, features Britney by the boardwalk contemplating a lost love. Considering she had recently hurt her knee, the dance scenes on the boardwalk are fairly demanding. While '… Baby One More Time' was a racier video, 'Sometimes' tried to present a softer, more innocent side of Britney. She wears all white in most of the scenes and her hair and make-up are subtle.

Britney's video for '(You Drive Me) Crazy' was her biggest yet, production-wise. It was also her most exhausting to shoot because she had so much going on: a live show the day of the video, and MTV was on the set shooting a documentary about the making of the video. True to Britney's personality, she remained calm and got the job done. The shoot took place in a converted warehouse in Los Angeles, made to look like a retro diner with green and red neon signs, rollerblading waitresses and lots of extras dancing in the background. The video also included cameo appearances by Melissa Joan Hart and Adrian Grenier, who starred in the romance comedy *Drive Me Crazy*.

Fans liked the up-tempo song and the high-energy dancing, and the video became yet another MTV fave.

Following the flashing lights and explosions of 'Crazy' was the sweet ballad 'From the Bottom of My Broken Heart'. The video, awash in sunflowers, swings and plenty of greenery was given the same soft glow by its director, Gregory Dark, as he gave to Mandy Moore's ballet-inspired video 'I Wanna Be With You'.

Filmed in a Los Angeles suburb, Britney's fourth US video features a hat-clad Britney displaying remarkable thespian powers as she tells the story of a girl who has to leave her family and boyfriend to go to college. Britney alternates the pace of her videos, going from up-tempo to ballad in a smooth succession. To make the point, 'From the Bottom Of My Broken Heart' was followed by the loud, fast, 'Oops! … I Did It Again', which certainly proved to be her most challenging video effort yet.

For this first single from her new album, she was determined to present a far-out video to accompany the edgy, electric sounds of 'Oops! … I Did It Again'. So she called the director Nigel Dick once more, to work his magic the way he had for '… Baby One More Time'. The now highly sought-after director has said that Britney just called him up one day and told him exactly what she had in mind for the video. She envisioned a space-age feel for her new video, which was to be set on another planet, specifically the fiery, tempestuous Mars. She also requested that the video feature a cute guy who would star as her counterpart, and she suggested there be no spaceships. The director also had to work in the *Titanic* dialogue, which on the album is actually Britney and Max Martin speaking. The British director homed in on the space-age themes to create one of the most multi-layered video productions ever.

Britney worked with the choreographer Tina Landin, who has supplied her with fabulous dance sequences in the past. Always her own stuntwoman, Britney herself supplied the awe-inspiring back flips and spinning.

In mid-March of 2000, Britney and crew met at Universal Studios in Studio City, California, where they would work from 16 to 18 March to make the video. Most videos take a maximum of two days to complete, so fans knew they could expect an elaborate video due to the extra day. The crew had no idea how much work would be involved and what strange events would unfold. At least the crew didn't know, but Britney had a hunch. She has said that she has good instincts and had a gut feeling something wasn't right when she woke up to work on the video that day. In fact, she felt drowsy as she was getting ready but didn't want to slow down the production. They had to finish the video that day and they were already behind schedule. But now we're getting ahead of our story.

Costumes are always important in a video, so Britney wanted to wear an eye-catching vinyl catsuit in candy-apple red to play on the fiery aspect of Mars. She also wanted retro hair and make-up, like Heather Graham in *Austin Powers: The Spy Who Shagged Me.* Her long, blonde, highlighted locks required time-intensive hair extensions, and the make-up look was achieved with 1960s-inspired psychedelic blue eye shadow (Britney loves blue). Just when everything seemed to be set, and she was in full costume trying out her dance steps for the camera, Britney noticed something wasn't right.

Her outfit turned out to be more problematic than she predicted. The tight catsuit flattened her front so much that stylists had to insert fake, padded breasts into the suit. With every turn that Britney made, the padding would slip lower and lower until the breasts would fall down, so she frequently had to take a break from shooting so the stylists could sew the padding in place. Then, she realized that vinyl is in fact very hot to wear, so after hours and hours of redoing her dance steps over and over for the camera, Britney noticed that as she did a spin or any type of movement with her arm, sweat would spray out of the bottom of her sleeves. This wasn't exactly the special effect she was looking for, so adjustments had to be made.

The scariest part of the shoot occurred during a complicated scene. For one shot, Britney had to lie down under an overhead camera that would zoom in and out. As she looked up, a big metal piece from the camera fell five feet and hit her on the head. She was knocked out, but when she came to she still insisted on continuing with the shot. It wasn't until a member of the crew saw blood that Britney realized she was actually bleeding from the head and needed to be checked out. A doctor was called to the set and Britney ended up needing four stitches. Because of the effects of concussion she began to feel sick, so the workaholic finally took a rest for about four hours.

Nigel Dick has said that he hopes an accident like that never happens again on his set. He shut down production for a few hours while Britney got help – and some rest – so she could continue. Britney is a trooper who would rather spend the time and energy getting the job done than to feel sorry for herself.

A lot was riding on Britney's shoulders during the shoot. She knew she had to catch a flight the next morning at 4.30 to make another performance, so they had to finish the video that day. Plus, during all the chaos after the accident, the set was full of random reporters and cameramen covering the behind-the-scenes shooting of the video. Even MTV's team was there, filming every detail, including the accident. Fortunately, the MTV producers decided against showing Britney's injury on their show. With all this activity, the now exhausted and injured Britney burst into tears. She has said that a good cry can be cathartic and actually makes her feel totally better. After a cry she asked for a massage, which cleared her mind and

rejuvenated her. She also had a mochaccino, which is one of her fave energy-boosting drinks, to keep her going.

Having fought the frazzled state she was in, Britney got back to work, stitches and all, and finished the video around 1 a.m. – three and a half hours before she had to catch her plane. She has said that she got back to the hotel at 2 a.m., took all her hair extensions and make-up off and had about one hour of sleep before hopping on the plane to get to her performance. Because Britney's afraid of flying, she didn't get much sleep on the plane either. She said that her performance for the show the next day ended up being a winner because, for a change, she directed the remainder of her dwindling energies towards her singing instead of her dancing.

Against all the odds, Britney once again delivered a dynamite video that scaled the top of the video countdown.

For international fans, Britney then released 'Born to Make You Happy', which was directed by Billy Woodruff, who also made Backstreet Boys' 'I'll Never Break Your Heart'.

Luckily, Britney's second video from the *Oops! … I Did It Again* album went smoothly. On 12 June she drove to Ren-Mar studios in Hollywood, parked her black convertible and got to work on her first day of shooting the video for the poignant song 'Lucky'. The director, David Meyers, envisioned the video to be set in the glamorous 1940s, so Britney wore an old Hollywood-inspired organza nightgown with a long robe, lined with boa feathers. Her hair was styled to look like Veronica Lake, an actress from the 1940s famous for her wavy locks that covered half of her face. At one point in the video, Britney gets up on a billboard wearing a red top and white pants. Her character, Lucky, has a scene with a handsome English guy, played by the actor Nathan James; Britney has said that she likes guys with accents. After lots of hard work, with several different set backgrounds and costume changes, the first day of shooting ended at 2.26 a.m. It was back to work the next day for more costume changes and new make-up looks. Britney has gorgeous pink, sparkling eye shadow on her lids in a few scenes, but, during one particularly dramatic scene, her face is smeared with black mascara to make it look like she's crying. Her character, Lucky, is supposed to be sad and lonely because of the isolating effects of stardom. This fictional character portrays feelings not unlike those that affect Britney from time to time. When asked if she relates to the song, Britney has said in a lot of ways she does. However, she doesn't like it when celebrities complain about their lives.

Britney has said she wouldn't trade her life for anything. She's happy, but does admit there are times when she has bad days, just like everybody else, and sometimes you can be very lonely even when you are surrounded by tons of people.

By 1.28 a.m. the video was complete and Britney, being the loyal older sister that she is, was free to catch the next plane home to Kentwood to see her sister dance.

A Fan of Fashion

When baby Brinnie wasn't dashing off to dance class or pursuing talent-show trophies, she would be in her playhouse, sometimes for six hours at a time, dressing her Barbies in all the new doll fashions. Even back then she loved clothes and spent hours with her cousin Laura Lynne playing dress-up in her mother's outfits. In the popular 'Got Milk?' ads, Britney is featured alongside another image of herself when she was a kid, wearing a gold lamé tutu. The pro-dairy ad was splashed all over magazines and newspapers, reminding us subtly that even when she was knee-high Britney was aware of her outfits.

She has said that she laughs when she sees old photos that capture her outdated outfits. She grew up in much of the 1980s and early 1990s, so acid-wash jeans, flannel shirts and jumpsuits with big patches were considered the ultimate fashion statement back then. She even remembers her mother dressing her up in a dress for her big *Star Search* performance that looked so puffy she could have flown away in it.

Growing up, she liked collecting hats – and has over twenty special styles in different designs and sizes in her closet. She still likes getting dolled up in dressy outfits, but now she's experimenting with an array of wild new styles that are inspired by the millennium, such as vinyl pants, metal-mesh tank tops and studded leather wrist bands.

Taking a tip from Madonna, Britney likes experimenting with different fashion styles. A decade ago, Madonna inspired her own blend of trends when she wore shoulder-revealing cut-off shirts, neon net vests and plastic bracelets up her arm. Britney knows it's crucial to constantly update and modify your wardrobe to stay on top of the trends and surprise fans. One thing's for sure:

Britney's fans will never be bored because this girl's got a passion for fashion that won't die.

Some critics have called her outfits too revealing, especially her belly-baring school uniform in '… Baby One More Time' or her two-piece outfit on her first cover of *Rolling Stone*. Britney sticks by her philosophy that you should wear what makes you happy and be comfortable with yourself. Britney has said that her mother brought her up to believe you should never be ashamed of your body because it's a beautiful thing.

Whether she's slithering into a snakeskin miniskirt and matching jacket – which she wore for her eighteenth birthday – or pulling on comfy sweatpants, which she wears most weekends, Britney knows when it's time to dress up or dress down. For award shows, Britney has an eye for glamorous get-ups that scream 'gorgeous!', like the silver pantsuit she wore at the American Music awards, which was a Chloe

original designed by Stella McCartney, daughter of the Beatles' Paul. Britney confesses that she wore double-sided tape to keep the top firmly secured. She also won praise from fashion aficionados when she wore the body-hugging, floor-length white dress for the Grammys.

This midriff-showing star has made her famous tummy even more famous with the addition of a silver and turquoise navel ring.

The fashion statement, which she had done while checking out the 'N Sync concert in Hawaii for Christmas 1999, hurt a lot, she has said. She also made a statement on her skin by getting a tattoo artist to design a black-winged fairy tattoo at the base of her spine. A hair stylist recommended a tattoo artist in New York City, so she went with her personal assistant, Fee, and her 300-pound bodyguard Rob to visit him in Manhattan's garment district, and picked out the fairy. Britney also wears several diamond-studded earrings.

Britney has started many trends with the cool costumes she wears in her videos. After '… Baby One More Time' debuted on MTV, thigh-high cotton stockings made a comeback, as did playfully pleated miniskirts. Trendsetting happens when an artist shows the world a new way to look at an old concept. Instead of tucking in her white cotton blouse for her first video, it was Britney's idea to tie up the shirt's ends into a knot so it would be easier to dance in – and cooler. This Southern girl points out that oversized T-shirts can be too hot to bust a move in. She often wears midriffs while she's performing because they keep her cool when she's sweating buckets from all the dancing. In fact, when she was criticized for wearing sport bras and midriffs, she replied that she's used to wearing light clothing because she's from the South and it gets unbearably hot. Britney likes to make a statement during her performances with fabulous fashion. For her Hawaiian concert, she wore a tummy-baring sarong and a turquoise beaded anklet to catch the spirit of the island.

Go on a shopping spree with Britney

If you ever get the chance to sneak Britney away from her busy tour for a shopping spree, you'd have a blast because this girl has an eye for spotting the trendiest threads in the store. You'd probably start your purchasing parade hunting for casual clothes at the Tommy Hilfiger store because Britney loves their comfy jeans and kick-back khakis. She was a 'Tommy girl' after all in 1999 when Tommy Hilfiger decided to sponsor her first ever headlining tour. Of course, it would be cool to pick up a few of Britney's clothes from her own fashion line, Britney Jeans. The catchy name is actually a witty play on Britney's first two names, Britney Jean (Jean is also the name of her grandmother).

Then your shopping marathon would bring you to Gap, Banana Republic and Abercrombie & Fitch for some more everyday clothes. Not one to skip sales, Britney would bring you right to the bargain racks to stock up on some staples such as crop tops and cotton drawstring pants, as seen in her video

'Sometimes'. Britney has said she likes to dress up but she also knows how great it is to be comfy in simple sweat pants. On her days off, comfortable, casual outfits are her first pick.

What are clothes without shoes? That's why your next stop with Britney would be at Skechers or Nike, where she picks up her rubber-soled sneakers for her action-packed concerts. Britney always takes extra care to wear shoes that support her ankles for non-stop dancing because she never wants to risk falling during a performance. It's impossible to do a back flip wearing slip-on sandals. Britney also likes the chunky designer shoes from Steve Madden and the durable leather boots from Nine West. Because she likes to appear taller than she is, Britney looks for heels to give her height. The best of both worlds would be comfy sneakers with rubber platform heels, like the ones she wears during her shows.

After a whirlwind of shopping for casual clothes, Britney would probably take you for a mini-break to gobble up an energy-boosting snack, like cookie-dough ice cream and a mug of frappachino. Then it's off to a few fancy stores for the party gowns Britney wears exclusively for special occasions – such as the 42nd Annual Grammy Awards. That stunning white dress was designed by Randolph Duke. While some of Britney's outfits have been custom-made by high-end designers, including Versace and Dolce & Gabbana, Britney also wears dresses found at accessible stores such as BCBG, Urban Outfitters, Betsey Johnson and Bebe. She also likes A/X Armani Exchange classic clothes.

If you happen to be in Chicago when Britney's in town, it's a safe bet you'll find the clothes queen checking out the new selections at Sugar Magnolia at 34 East Oak Street, an address Britney knows by heart. No matter how busy her day is, if she happens to be stopping in the windy city, she always finds time to browse her fave store for innovative, creative outfits.

She also loves the shopping in Manhattan and says New Yorkers have a wild sense of style that she wouldn't be able to wear in her hometown without turning heads. She has said that skirts that hit below the knee aren't flattering, so she prefers skirts with slits or miniskirts.

Hair and Make-up Tricks

Britney has a blast trying out new beauty concepts in front of the mirror. She remembers rummaging through her mother's make-up case when she was a kid, trying out all the blushes, lipsticks and eye shadows she could find. Of course, she never left the house that way, but she learned early on that she enjoyed experimenting with beauty products.

Britney remembers one make-up artist on *The New Mickey Mouse Club* telling her she was too young to be concerned with wearing make-up off the set. Since then, she's learned lots of tricks just from watching the professionals who style her hair and make-up for concerts, award shows, and photo shoots. She has learned how to sweep her eyelids with subtle peach instead of gobbing on waxy black liner, and she now treats her hair to deep protein conditioners and shine-boosting serums.

Britney has experimented with different hair lengths, but her biggest change happened during an *Allure* magazine cover shoot.

She had been wearing long, blonde hair extensions until she decided to lighten her head load with a choppy bob.

The short cut, best highlighted in her video 'Lucky', was a hit. Britney will continue to try new looks and has even taken to wearing wigs during her shows. To get her fake head of hair just right, a stylist has to flatten her locks with plastic and strip tape over her head. After the fake strands are woven into the base, the wig is returned to Britney for her to try. Although it sounds less than glamorous, once Britney puts on the final product she has instant, stay-put tresses for her performance. Then, when she's done with the show, she just swipes off the wig and goes back to her natural length.

Although Britney has a permanent tattoo, she still likes to decorate her hands with temporary henna tattoos in the shape of little flowers. The highly reputable beauty brand, Clairol, asked Britney to be their 'spokes-star' for their Herbal Essences hair line. Britney has said she likes their shampoos because they keep her hair healthy. Clairol sponsored her 'Oops! … I Did It Again' tour.

Britney often appears polished and camera-ready but she hasn't escaped her share of embarrassing beauty moments. She remembers the time she unintentionally accentuated a huge pimple on her face.

That's right, instead of hiding it with concealer, she emphasized it with glitter. Unbeknown to her, a jar of glitter had spilled in her make-up bag, mixing with her concealer, so when she tried to cover up her blemish she only drew more attention to it. She has also had haircuts that made her want to hide, and botched dye jobs that turned her naturally light-brown locks orange. Just like any girl on the planet, Britney likes to look good, so she flips through beauty magazines and chats with girlfriends to learn new hair and make-up ideas. Here are some star-studded beauty solutions that even pop stars want to learn.

Beauty Q&A

(1) **Q: How can I add more volume to my hair?**

A: *Use a volumizing product and blow-dry your locks upside down, aiming the hot air at your roots. These tips help Britney, who has said she wishes she had thicker hair.*

(2) **Q: How can I score a clearer complexion?**

A: *The trick to getting skin flawless is to work from the inside out. Fame for Britney means her face gets photographed a lot, and all during the height of her teenage years when her skin isn't always its clearest. So to fight blemishes – yep, even stars get pimples – she always washes off her make-up before she goes to sleep no matter how tired she is. Britney also drinks plenty of water, which helps purify your skin.*

(3) **Q: My teeth aren't as bright as I'd like. What can I do?**

A: *Good teeth are in your genes, but you can help nature by taking extra care of them. Britney had braces for a couple of years, which helped straighten her teeth. For a pearly white smile, pop stars know it's best to avoid teeth-staining foods like tomato sauce, coffee and soda.*

(4) **Q: How can I bring out my eyes?**

A: *Britney has naturally big, wide-set eyes, but even so she accentuates their size by lightly plucking her eyebrows. After a hot shower, lightly tweeze stray hairs below your brow bone. Remember a trick Britney's make-up artists have told her: never overpluck.*

(5) **Q: How do I get my hair to look longer?**

A: *This is an easy one. Either wait for it to grow or, more simply, attach hair extensions as Britney does. After she cut her hair, Britney still wanted it to look longer during her shows, so she adds blonde extensions.*

(6) **Q: How can I make my lipstick last?**

A: *When Britney needs the effect to last during a show, she chooses a long-lasting lipstick from MAC. Another way to make your pout perfect is to apply foundation on your lips before gliding on lipstick. Britney also lines her lips with a shade that matches her lipstick for extra definition.*

(7) Q: How can I get a healthy glow?

A: *Lots of exercise and running back and forth on stage during a performance keeps Britney's heart racing, her blood pumping and her cheeks rosy. You can dust your cheeks with bronzing powder. Or, if you want to go a little further, you can try one of Britney's beauty weaknesses: self-tanner. The trick to getting self-tanner to look even is to exfoliate your skin first, wash your hands during the application so they don't turn orange, and do your knees and elbows last because they stick out and look darker anyway.*

(8) Q: How do I make my high forehead look smaller?

A: *High foreheads are a sign of beauty, but, if you really feel you want to diminish the size, you can make it appear smaller by adding a light fringe or wisps to frame your face, like Britney does.*

(9) Q: How can I stay stress-free?

A: *When Britney is having a hectic day, which is pretty much all the time, she treats herself to a relaxing bubble bath, using aromatherapy gels. She also plays soothing music and lights candles.*

(10) Q: What's the best way for wide-open eyes?

A: *If you have been studying hard for a test and want to hide your red eyes the next morning, try this trick from the star stylists. Line the inside of your eyelids with white eyeliner.*

(11) Q: How do you get hair to shine?

A: *Britney's tresses keep their shine with conditioners, shine-enhancing serums and natural boar-bristle brushes. Also, rinsing hair with cold water seals the hair cuticle and pumps up the shining power.*

(12) Q: I have a habit of biting my nails. How can I stop and let them grow?

A: *Britney has the nail-chomping habit, so to save her tips she has started to wear fake nails over her real nails to break the habit.*

(13) Q: Are there some stay-fit tips?

A: *Britney has been finding inner peace and extra flexibility from yoga classes. Yoga is fast becoming a frequent pastime with stars such as Gwyneth Paltrow and Jennifer Aniston. She also tries to do three hundred sit-ups every day. She has said that, when she went running a lot, her legs got too big and she looked like a bodybuilder, so she exercises in moderation.*

(14) Q: What are some easy ways to dress up without lots of make-up?

A: *When Britney's on the go, she swipes clear gloss over her lips for a natural look. You can also try clear mascara or soft frosty shadow on your eyelids.*

(15) Q: How do I grab that gorgeous lash look?

A: *Opt for waterproof mascara. It's a fave for pop stars who want to avoid make-up mess-ups from sweaty performances. In the 'Lucky' video, Britney's mascara is purposely smudged, but usually she keeps her lashes intact.*

chapter

nine

Giving Back

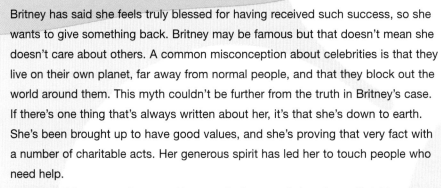

Britney has said she feels truly blessed for having received such success, so she wants to give something back. Britney may be famous but that doesn't mean she doesn't care about others. A common misconception about celebrities is that they live on their own planet, far away from normal people, and that they block out the world around them. This myth couldn't be further from the truth in Britney's case. If there's one thing that's always written about her, it's that she's down to earth. She's been brought up to have good values, and she's proving that very fact with a number of charitable acts. Her generous spirit has led her to touch people who need help.

When Britney goes home to Kentwood, she spends her days off visiting cancer patients at local hospitals. She has said the experience brings tears to her eyes and it cleanses her spirit.

Britney has also been working with the Starlight Children's Foundation to create hospital playrooms around the USA.

She launched the first one at Chicago's Shriners Hospital for Children. The room will be a recreation area for teen patients undergoing long-term care.

For the Arthur Ashe Kids' Day at the US Open in New York, Britney sang and performed with her dancers while other celebrities, such as the MTV VJ Carson Daly, also contributed to the day's events. Britney participated in Scholastic's Read for 2000, a campaign to inspire thousands of students to pick up books and read for 2,000 seconds (or 33.33 minutes).

She has also performed at Nickelodeon's 'Big Holiday Help-a-thon' with other artists such as 'N Sync and Puff Daddy to increase awareness about teen volunteerism. She appeared on the television game show *Hollywood Squares* to raise money for charity and donated an imprint of her lips for an AIDS research organization in New York. Madonna, Rosie O'Donnell, Shania Twain and others donated their puckered mouths for the cause, too.

Britney posed for MTV's '*TRL* Grammy Class of 2000 Poster' with a bunch of other artists including Limp Bizkit, Jennifer Lopez and Christina Aguilera. Sales from the poster benefited various charities which fund music education classes in schools and help MTV's anti-violence campaign 'Fight For Your Rights: Take A

Stand Against Violence'. She also volunteered her voice on Pope John Paul II's album *World Voice 2000*, which was released by Columbia Records in 2000. She joined 'N Sync, Monica, 98 Degrees, Jennifer Love Hewitt and others reciting the Pope's prayers.

Britney has also started her own foundation as well, to give inner-city schoolchildren the chance to study performing arts. She remembers all the training she received growing up and wants other kids to get the same opportunity. Her foundation teamed up with Giving Back Fund, a national not-for-profit organization, to create a unique summer camp for kids. The camp provides the best acting coaches, vocal coaches and training possible. It opened up during the summer of 2000 and the feedback was outstanding. Britney hand-picked 85 lucky kids who were put up at an all-expenses-paid countryside camp in the gorgeous Berkshire mountains of western Massachusetts for two weeks in August. It was hard to narrow down the search, but in the future there will be room for more kids. Britney's choreographer and singing coach shared their expertise with workshops; Britney will spend more time helping out next year. She's said that she thinks more kids should be exposed to the top-notch training she was able to get growing up.

Britney has also donated her time and energy to helping the Humane Society of the United States, which is an organization that protects the welfare of animals. As her fans already know, Britney is an animal lover.

She and her family own several dogs, Mitzy, Bitzy, Lady and Cane. Mitzy was a Christmas present from her parents.

When the dog was potty-trained, Britney brought the pint-sized Teacup Yorkshire Terrier on her travels and has said that after a show, no matter how good or bad it went, her little dog was always there to provide affection. She is also partial to her younger sister's dog, Bitzy, which she has nicknamed Baby and Boo-Boo. Aside from dogs, Britney has a soft spot for dolphins, and had the chance to swim with the gentle creatures when she visited Hawaii. Britney likes all things that are small and cute, including kids. She says that, when she's older and married, she would like to have three or four kids, hopefully around the same time as her best friend Laura Lynne.

chapter ten

Fast-Forward To The Future

If you think the past couple of years have been eventful for Britney, wait until you see what this busy girl has planned for the future. For starters, she is already planning her third album, and hopes to devote at least six months to it. That would be the longest amount of time Britney's worked on an album. She also plans on writing more songs after the success of 'Dear Diary' and says she has started learning the guitar to improve her songwriting skills. Britney has been thinking up melodies non-stop – usually while relaxing in the bathtub – and surprisingly, she says, they resemble those of Macy Gray and Sheryl Crow rather than traditional pop.

If it's a case of 'three times lucky', then this next studio effort could even top … *Baby One More Time* and *Oops! … I Did It Again.* Britney has said she would also like to put together a movie like Madonna's *Truth Or Dare*, incorporating her dancers to capture her life on tour.

Along with pursuing her own creative projects, Britney has been asked to collaborate with other artists, namely her good friends from 'N Sync. The idea is for Britney to sing a duet with the guys for their next album, and, according to the group's Lance Bass, the song could quite possibly be the hottest ever.

Along the lines of Janet Jackson and Michael Jackson's duet 'Scream', the Britney/'N Sync collaboration would be edgy and dance oriented.

Britney may also join 'N Sync on the big screen for a movie similar to Britney's self-confessed fave flick, *The Bodyguard*, starring Whitney Houston and Kevin Costner. The romance/comedy could start production as early as the beginning of 2001. Movie scripts have been landing at Britney's feet since she first hit the scene; she has said that she would absolutely love to pursue acting when her music career allows the time for it. Some movie possibilities have included Britney starring in several sequels, such as *Grease 3* and *Dirty*

Dancing 2, as well as the actor Jerry O'Connell's self-penned upcoming movie, *First Daughter.* Britney would play a rebellious daughter of the President of the United States.

Britney may also land the main role as Alice in MTV Films' updated movie version of Lewis Carroll's classic tale *Alice's Adventures in Wonderland.* The modernized script has Alice walking through a city only to be hit by a Volkswagen Rabbit and thrown into an imaginative world where hip-hop and rock 'n' roll music is played. The producers envision Ricky Martin to play the role of the Mad Hatter. Although Britney has been too busy touring to devote herself to a movie, and has had to turn roles down, such as a possible spot in *Scary Movie,* she is now ready to expand her career to include all genres – music, television and movies.

Professionally, Britney will still be busy, but she's said she plans to spend more time on her personal life. That means more trips back home to see her family and watch her younger sister, Jamie Lynn, grow up. This family girl puts her priorities first and has proven that you can be a private person in a public world and still stay grounded. Aside from confirming her place in the musical history books, Britney has reminded each and every one of us that you can reach for the stars, and touch them. That you can have dreams and live them. That it's easy to forget the strength of your passions – you have to believe in yourself.

Quiz: Test your Britney Trivia

1 **Which video was Britney rehearsing for when she twisted her knee?**

   a. '... Baby One More Time'

   b. 'Sometimes'

   c. 'Lucky'

2 **Where did Britney get her fairy tattoo?**

   a. London

   b. Kentwood

   c. New York

3 **Which song did Britney sing for her audition with Jive?**

   a. Whitney Houston's 'I Have Nothing'

   b. Mariah Carey's 'Vision of Love'

   c. Madonna's 'Material Girl'

4 **Which celebrity was not on *The New Mickey Mouse Club* with Britney?**

   a. Keri Russell

   b. Tony Lucca

   c. Joshua Jackson

5 **How old was Britney when she was photographed for her first album *... Baby One More Time*?**

   a. 12

   b. 15

   c. 17

6 **What is Britney scared of?**

   a. animals

   b. performing

   c. flying in a plane

7 **Who makes a guest appearance in Britney's video 'Drive Me Crazy'?**

   a. Melissa Joan Hart

   b. Adrian Grenier

   c. Christina Aguilera

8 **Which group did Britney open for in late 1998?**

   a. Backstreet Boys

   b. Spice Girls

   c. 'N Sync

9 **Which group originally recorded '(I Can't Get No) Satisfaction', before Britney?**

   a. Aerosmith

   b. Rolling Stones

   c. Eagles

10 **Which song did Britney and her mother sing in the car that Britney later performed in concert?**

   a. Journey's 'Open Arms'

   b. Madonna's 'Like a Prayer'

   c. Bette Midler's 'Wind Beneath My Wings'

11 Who did Britney call when she won at the American Music Awards?

a. her manager

b. her mother

c. Carson Daly

12 How many awards did Britney win at the MTV European music awards?

a. 2

b. 3

c. 4

13 Who directed her video 'Oops! ... I Did It Again'?

a. Gregory Dark

b. Stephen Spielberg

c. Nigel Dick

14 What video did Britney shorten to two days' filming instead of three so she could see her sister's dance recital?

a. 'Lucky'

b. 'From the Bottom of My Broken Heart'

c. '... Baby One More Time'

15 What do most fans wave in the air at Britney's concerts?

a. flags

b. posters

c. glow sticks

16 Who did Britney meet for dinner at Planet Hollywood in Los Angeles?

a. Brad Pitt

b. Enrique Iglesias

c. Ben Affleck

17 Britney's astrological sign is:

a. Sagittarius

b. Aquarius

c. Leo

18 What candy does Britney especially like and keep on her tour bus?

a. giant lollipops

b. chocolate bars

c. mints

19 Where did Britney spend her eighteenth-birthday party?

a. a New York club

b. her tour bus

c. in Kentwood

20 What has helped Britney realize her dreams?

a. the support of her family

b. her fans loyalty

c. her own dedication and drive

Answers: 1. b; **2.** c; **3.** a; **4.** c; **5.** b; **6.** c; **7.** a & b; **8.** c; **9.** b; **10.** a; **11.** b; **12.** c; **13.** c; **14.** a; **15.** c; **16.** c; **17.** a; **18.** a; **19.** a; **20.** all of them

Discography

Singles

'... Baby One More Time'
Jive, released November 1998

'... Baby One More Time'
BMG International, released February 1999
Highest Chart Position: 1

'Sometimes'
Jive, released April 1999
Highest Chart Position: 14

'Crazy'
Jive, released September 1999
Highest Chart Position: 10

'From the Bottom of My Broken Heart'
Jive, released February 2000
Highest Chart Position: 14

'Oops! ... I Did It Again'
Jive, released May 2000
Highest Chart Position: 9

'Lucky'
Jive, released August 2000

Albums

Oops! ... I Did It Again
Jive, released 16 May 2000
Highest Chart Position: 1
Tracks: 'Oops! ... I Did It Again', 'Stronger', Don't Go Knockin' On My Door', '(I Can't Get No) Satisfaction', 'Don't Let Me Be the Last To Know', 'What U See (Is What U Get)', 'Lucky', 'One Kiss From You', 'Where Are You Now', 'Can't Make You Love Me', 'When Your Eyes Say It', 'Dear Diary'

... Baby One More Time
Jive, released January 1999
Highest Chart Position: 1

... Baby One More Time
BMG International, released February 1999
Highest chart position: 1
Tracks: '... Baby One More Time', '(You Drive Me) Crazy', 'Sometimes', 'Soda Pop', 'Born To Make You Happy', 'From the Bottom of My Broken Heart', 'I Will Be There', 'I Will Still Love You', 'Thinkin' About You', 'E-mail My Heart', 'The Beat Goes On'

Write to Britney:

The Britney Beat
PO Box 192730
San Francisco, CA 94119-2730

Or visit her website at:

www.britney.com and www.britneyspears.com